INSERT

Author's Note

This book would not have come into being without the vision and encouragement of my wife Shirley. It represents our nearly sixty years of pilgrimage together, in South Africa, Wales, and England. In detail, it owes much to her candid and creative judgements, especially in the suggestions of questions for study and for working groups.

I am very grateful to Archbishop Barry Morgan for his enthusiastic Foreword, his nomination of the book as the Archbishop of Wales's Lent Book 2016, for his approval of the Dedication to the Church in Wales Mobile Dental Clinic in Gaza, and for his encouragement and suggestions for the text.

And thank you to Archdeacon Philip Morris, the main link-person with the Gaza project from the Welsh side, for the information which he has supplied about this courageous, visionary and very practical enterprise.

Although the book is commended by the Archbishop of Wales, and is written from within a Welsh context, I hope that it can have some usefulness for people who don't have the good fortune to live within the Principality. We ourselves have, for the last fourteen years, lived in England in Shropshire, four miles from the border, in the special and interesting area known as *y Gororau,* the Marches. During that time, most of my commitments as a minister have been in Wales, under the authority of the Bishop of St Asaph; for this, I am truly grateful to him. But I am also grateful to the Vicar of our Parish of Gobowen, for his generous acceptance of me as a colleague. The book owes much to recent experience in both areas.

I am grateful to Professor John Rogerson and Dr John Vincent, who have been the main coordinators and editors of the Practice Interpretation series of studies, for their encouragement and their willingness to accept this book as a somewhat odd kind of specimen within the Practice

Interpretation species; and to Dr David Orton of Deo Publishing, the publishers of the previous works of this series, for his encouragement and acceptance of the book within the series.

Thanks also to Bishop Michael Bourke for his encouragement and helpful suggestions, particularly concerning the Martin Luther references

I am grateful to Gwasg Gomer, Llandysul, for permission to include the quotations of 14 lines from Saunders Lewis *Buchedd Garmon* and two lines from Gwenallt *Eples*.

Thanks also to the sculptor Ian Rank-Broadley, for his agreement to the inclusion of the picture of part of his great work at the Armed Forces Memorial.

Gladstone's Library, Hawarden, has been a valuable resource for in-dentifying and consulting other work in this field; and I am grateful to it for giving a secure home to my precious recording of Martin Luther King's lecture of 1964.

For our concluding Affirmation of Faith, I am glad to acknowledge debt to Desmond Tutu, friend and colleague in the 1960s.

Finally, heartfelt thank you to groups of people over the last fifty years, students in South Africa and Birmingham, congregations in Llanrhaeadr ym Mochnant and Gobowen, and many others, who have thought and talked and prayed with me on the themes of this book.

This book is dedicated to the Church in Wales Mobile Dental Clinic in Gaza; all profits due to the author will go to that project.

JOHN D DAVIES
Epiphany 2016, Gobowen

Three Mountains to Freedom
Practice Interpretation of Paul's Letter to the Galatians

Practice Interpretation

5

ISSN 2048-0431

Series Editor
John Vincent

Deo Publishing

THREE MOUNTAINS
to FREEDOM

John Dudley Davies

deo
PUBLISHING

BLANDFORD FORUM

Practice Interpretation series, 5

ISSN 2048-0431

Editorial address:
Practice Interpretation
Urban Theology Unit, Victoria Hall, Norfolk Street, Sheffield S1 2JB

Please contact the editor for information on forthcoming meetings of the
Practice Interpretation group.

Printed by Henry Ling Ltd, at the Dorset Press, Dorchester, DT1 1HD, UK

British Library Cataloguing-in-Publication data
A catalogue record for this book is available from the British Library

ISBN 978-1-905679-35-5

Contents

Contents

Foreword

In the most recent Confirmation Service of the Church in Wales, there is a new addition. The Bishop addresses every candidate individually and says *"God has called you by name and made you his own."* For me, as the confirming bishop, it is one of the most striking and wonderful things that is said, since it makes it clear that God calls all manner of people to follow him and that our calling does not depend on our goodness, our status, our job, education, wealth or anything else. In theological short hand, we are called and accepted by God simply through grace. Yet, although that is the heart of the Gospel, I am constantly astonished at the number of Christians who do not seem either to realise or believe that that is the case. They think they have to earn that grace or can never deserve it (but that's the whole point) and find it hard to accept that love is God's defining characteristic as shown in the person of Jesus Christ. This book on virtually every page makes clear in a host of different ways that the heart of the Gospel is about *"The Son of God who loved me and gave himself for me."*

In his letter to the Galatians, St Paul expounds that message clearly as he writes to a particular community at a particular time about their particular problems. They were Gentiles who needed to be reassured that they did not have to or need to become Jews in order to become Christians, for Christ had set them free from that necessity. But as the author shows, the central message of Paul to the Galatians applies to our very different circumstances as we grapple with issues of race, gender, poverty and inequality. God sets us free from having to prove ourselves, for all of us are his children. Reading scripture intelligently enables us to see the relevance of this letter to our own lives with its different problems. John Davies makes Paul immensely accessible, unfolding meaty theology and New Testament scholarship with the lightest of touches, seasoned and informed by anecdotes from ministry in the UK and South Africa during the apartheid regime, a ministry which was clearly very courageous and costly.

The book has some wonderful one-liners, including: "The Gospel does not come to abolish conflict, but to convert conflict into tension; creativity does not spread out neatly in ripples from the centre to the edge, it often begins on the edge; faith is the propellant which moves you out of your comfort zone; if you find a church which suits you, the chances are you have found a god who suits you; better to have a vision with inconsistencies than to have consistency without the vision; baptism, if it is insignia at all, is the insignia of those who renounce insignia; the Gospel's simple secret is that you join God by getting wet; a police state is not state in which there are crowds of obvious policemen at every street corner, it is a state in which many members of the public have allowed themselves to become unpaid and un-uniformed policemen." And his discursus on disability on page 52 has an exquisite eloquence worthy of a spiritual classic.

The author hopes this book will make a difference to those who study it, either individually or in a group. Too often we study the Bible and it has no impact on the way we live our lives. Yet the word of God is always an "incarnate word" – having implications for all that we are and do if we but open our eyes and ears to what the scriptures have to say to us. This book is full of insights about the ways in which our 'blinded sight' can be flooded with light so that saved by grace we can also try to live by it in a world that is totally different from that of either Jesus or Paul. I am delighted to commend it as my Lent book for 2016, knowing full well that it is a book that will repay pondering at any time.

Dr Barry Morgan
Archbishop of Wales

Introduction

'The Englishman who went up a hill but came down a mountain'. A clever and successful movie in 1995; it was claimed as a Welsh film, centring on the issue of whether a certain feature in the landscape was only a hill, or whether it was high enough to qualify for the title of a 'mountain'. It was supposed to be about Garth Mountain, near Ffynnon Tâf, in South Wales; but it was actually made on location in Llanrhaeadr ym Mochnant, 90 miles further north (where I was once the vicar). The village provided some of the cast.

What is a mountain? The debate in the film was based on the ruling that a hill could be a mountain only if it was one thousand or more feet high. I want to suggest a slightly different definition. From the top of a hill, you can see other hills. From the top of a mountain you can see the world.

This book is a reading of the letter which Saint Paul wrote to his friends, the members of the Christian church in Galatia. He was writing quite soon after the crucifixion and resurrection of Jesus – probably only about 23 years after, and an even shorter time after his own conversion to Christ.

His letter is not a carefully worked-out thesis, not a booklet of organised doctrine. It is, like most letters, written to specific readers, in a specific place, for a specific purpose, to respond to a specific situation. In fact, nowhere else in his writings is Paul so definitely local. He has to deal with a specific problem, and deal with it in specific ways.

So, for a lot of the time, he is, as it were, scrambling about the foothills, trying to find a message that will click with these specific people. But, every now and then, he gets to the top of a hill and finds that it is a mountain; he finds a message that gives signals across the valleys, across the oceans, across the centuries; a message that is alive and vigorous for us.

I call the three mountains of Paul's letter, Mount Faith/*Moel Ffydd*, Mount Unity/*Moel Undod*, Mount Freedom/*Moel Rhyddid*.

But, in giving these names, we are not implying that this terrain is reserved for professional mountaineers. You won't need crampons or ice-axes. Paul is not a lonely expert; he is hoping that ordinary people will be able to follow his example and find themselves seeing the views that he sees. For him, the way was not always easy, and sometimes his vision was limited.

We might usefully recall a story of a couple of tourists who set off to climb Snowdon; soon after leaving the Pen-y-Gwryd Hotel, they met a local shepherd, who noted that they were well equipped with sensible clothing and boots, had with them mobile phones and whistle and some food and drink, and carried compass and map. 'You'll do', he said; but added, 'Does your map show the mist?'

This book is not intended as a full commentary on Paul's Letter to the Galatians. It is an attempt at Practice Interpretation; the meaning of Scripture includes the effect that it has upon its readers and hearers. Its meaning is registered in the practical implications which it has, for specific situations and specific people. The sculptor Bridget Riley says: 'Someone who practices as an artist makes a work but does not make a work of art. This is done by others, by those who receive it.'[1] You can make a study of a book of the Bible, analyse its structure and work out its original meaning. You can organise and classify and make a scientific-style account of it. You can try to master it, control it, show that your understanding is correct and someone else's is incorrect. This can be very helpful, just as it will be necessary for a maker of tennis rackets to understand the properties of wood, glue, and cord. But the quality of tennis-racket manufacture is put into practice by the tennis-player, the person in the game.

In Practice Interpretation, we do not try to understand the Bible; we let the Bible stand over us. We let the text loose on our world; and this will never be complete or uniform. But it can add something to the total experience of our community across the centuries. The textual analysis of the book is not the meaning of the book for us; the meaning is in the impact that it makes on us, in our attempts to Practice what the book is about. When it is just the words, it is lifeless. For us, the word can become flesh; the word becomes incarnate. And, as the incarnation of the Son of God makes clear, incarnation means being at the mercy of the situation in which it happens.

This is what was happening for Paul; he had a message, which he could put into words. But he had to struggle to get that message to live and to be effective in a particular situation, to be received, to be incarnate. Without that, it would be mere formula. Bridget Riley's account of the artist's work can apply exactly to Paul's work. Paul writes a letter, for a specific time and place; it is for others to react to it, to recognise its wider value, and to incorporate it, with many other contributions, into that collection of insights which we call the New Testament. It was the task of a long series of committees and councils to decide what texts should be included in the New Testament. There was inspiration in their work, just as much as there was in the work of the original writers. There should be a Festival to commemorate editors! They had to struggle to select and decide what is significant for a readership much wider than the original, way beyond what the original writer had in mind. So we, in our turn, need to struggle to recognise what is valid for us, in our situation. That is Practice Interpretation.

So this is an invitation to you to get involved with what Paul has written, and to see where it takes you. It was written for a purpose, and that purpose includes you. What do you make of it? And what does it make of you? It meant a lot to me and to my colleagues in the specific context of the Christian struggle against the apartheid ideology in South Africa; I believe that it can mean a lot in this country in the 21st century. I hope that you will find that it will mean a lot to you, where you are. But this will be for you to discover; what I have to offer may be helpful, or it may get in the way. What you make of it will be your responsibility.

Before you study Paul's Letter in detail, in the sections into which we divide it in this book, it would be best to read it straight through, to catch the sweep of the story as a whole. I call the sections of this book 'steps', simply to distinguish them from the 'chapters' into which Paul's letter is divided.

There are several recognised translations of the Bible into English; I have based this book on the New Revised Standard Version, which I think is in most ways the best. The Good News Bible is also widely used; it has the great advantage that it is best for those millions of people across the world for whom English is their ail–iaith, their second language. If you are working with other people in a group, it can be valuable if you bring a variety of versions, and share their insights; no single version is perfect.

The questions which are included here are only suggestions; don't be constrained by them, but let the text of the Letter lead you in the way that seems right to you. And before you get into the questions which we offer, take time to note your own personal responses, both to Paul's writing and to the chapters of this book. Your own interest and response to Paul's text have to come first.

Further, Paul was not writing just for the edification of isolated individuals; he was writing for the community, for the church, to help the church to discover its direction and purpose, to sift through its sense of identity and its calling, to weigh up its successes and failures, and especially to reckon with the meaning of Christ for its community-life. Where does this letter hit the life and conscience and hope of your church? This book is written to encourage that enquiry; I hope that the questions may help study-groups in local churches to renew their response to their calling.

This book is called a Lent Book. It certainly need not be limited to Lent; I hope that it will have a rather wider usefulness. But, if you are taking it as a study-course for Lent, you probably will wish to use it in five meetings. In that case, I suggest that you just read over Steps 3 and 5, along with the sections of Paul's Letter to which they refer, so as to keep the continuity; but base your meetings on the other five Steps.

A study-group needs to know *why* it is in business. Paul had a clear purpose in writing his Letter – to help the church to get its priorities right, in both its belief in Christ and in its life as a community. Too often, a parish church runs a study-group or a Lent course, which fulfils a programme but makes no difference to the public policy or practice of the church as a whole – let alone any difference to the world around. A study-group should feel accountable to the church for the time and energy which it puts into its efforts. It can see itself as a think-tank, or research team, or pressure-group. It will change and develop its members, so that they can help to change and develop the church, so that it can help to change and develop the world around. It will have a purpose.

In engaging with this study-programme, you are making yourself open to God's influence through the Scripture. No one can tell where this will lead – certainly the author of this book cannot. But I imagine that most groups who get into this sort of study will want to affirm and dedicate their thinking in prayer. For this reason, I offer some suggestions for Prayer and Thanksgiving at the end of each Step. These relate to some of the main themes of the study; but please do not be limited by them; they are only suggestions. Your prayer will be best if it arises directly from your own exchange of insights.

STEP 1

The first foothills of Paul's pilgrimage
Galatians 1:1-24

In the mid-1950s, when my wife and I first arrived to work in South Africa, there was one place in that land which was better-known across the world than all others. It was not a great industrial centre, or a beautiful park, or an area of splendid mansions. It was a chaotic slum, crowded with nigh-on 100,000 inhabitants, with tiny houses, shacks, shops, cinemas and shebeens. Sophiatown, the home of the families of Mandela and Tutu, of the singer Miriam Makeba and the trumpeter Hugh Masakele; an area of violence and crime, of passionate politics and exuberant culture, of hope, yearning, and despair.

It defied the relentless intrusion of the apartheid regime which could not tolerate its existence as the one large urban area where black people had freehold rights. The regime saw it as one huge blot on the landscape, which had to be obliterated.

Its most powerful landmark, standing high over this extraordinary scene, was the great Church of Christ the King; based there, Father Trevor Huddleston had been Sophiatown's parish priest, moving day by day from the altar in church to the soapbox in Freedom Square, encouraging the people's resistance to the policy of enforced removals. In a great arch of brickwork, over the main door of that church, there was inscribed the church's message to the world, the core-statement of St Paul's Letter to the Galatians: 'THE SON OF GOD WHO LOVED ME AND GAVE HIMSELF FOR ME.'

From the Letter to the Galatians, there are other texts which might well have served as headlines for the church's manifesto: 'All of you are one in Christ Jesus'; or, 'For freedom, Christ has set us free.' But the Church of Christ the King chose this message as its proclamation: 'The Son of God who loved me and gave himself for me.' This is the glorious song of Evangelical faith; but it is also the central personal assurance of the Mass in Catholic consciousness – 'the Body of our Lord Jesus Christ given for *You*'. And, as Paul's Letter makes clear, this text is the engine which gives most fundamental energy to our political sense of the un-

conditional value of each human being. It is the summit and the summary of the Gospel witness. It is Mount Faith, the first mountain-top in
St Paul's exploration.

Despite all the resistance, Sophiatown was doomed. By the early
1960s, the regime's policy had succeeded; almost all the houses and other
buildings had been destroyed, with just the streets left visible – the
Group Areas Act had been implemented and all the people had been
shifted miles away. Sophiatown was no more – the area had been re-
named as Triomf, the triumph of the ideology of apartheid. The Church
of Christ the King still stood, presiding over this waste-land, still with its
defiant message about the love of God, which politics could not totally
obliterate.

After another 40 years, in 2006, there was a new regime; Sophiatown
regained its old name. The Church of Christ the King, after several
changes of use, is back in business; its message remains as ever.

Paul's Letter to the Galatians is all about the relationship between three
places, three components of the diverse but single thing which is the
church of Jesus Christ. Almost every church is going to find that it has
to try to hold these three components together.

First, there was the group of churches to which Paul was writing,
people of Galatia, a state of the Roman Empire in what is now in Ana-
tolia, central Turkey; it was a mix of people of different backgrounds,
some slave, some free; some had been converts from Judaism, others
were Greek-speaking Gentiles, some had been pagan peasants who had
not had much contact with any other culture. The Romans called them
Galli, or Celts. So many of them could have been members of tribes of
the Celtic dispersion; Bishop Lightfoot, that learned and imaginative
Victorian scholar, speculated that when traders from western Britain met
Galatian people in the commerce of tin and spices, they would recognise
each other's languages. He, respected English academic that he was,
noted how Paul saw that the Galatians were passionate, excitable, enthusiastic, fickle, quarrelsome, unreliable – just like his Celtic neighbours
in the west![2] These were people who had gladly heard Paul's message,
the message of a Saviour sent from God to form a new community of
hope for all the world. They had had no need of the rites and systems of
Judaism. For them, as they at first understood Paul's preaching, any such
complications were unnecessary.

Secondly, there was the group of Christians in Jerusalem, the place
where Jesus himself had preached and lived and died and had risen again.
Like Jesus himself, they were Jews, and they still took their Jewish identity seriously. Nothing that Jesus had said suggested that they should stop
being Jewish or that the Jewish identity was something that they could

disregard. They were the guardians of the tradition, preserving the stories about Jesus, insisting that he was the fulfilment of the prophecies of the Hebrew scriptures. They were the 'Establishment'; but, unlike most Establishments, they were financially poor; they were paying the price for what the conventional Jews reckoned as a betrayal of their most precious traditions. They needed the support of the wealthier communities of the new churches.

And, thirdly, there was Antioch. If the Jerusalem group and the Galatian group never met, never had anything to do with each other, there would be no problem. But Antioch was the place of encounter and confusion. It was the city where the disciples of Jesus were first labelled as a specific community, the 'Christians'.[3] In Antioch, on the northern edge of modern Syria, there were Christians who were just as genuinely Jewish as their colleagues in Jerusalem; and there were Christians who were Gentiles, just as uninvolved with Jewish identity as their colleagues in Galatia. In Antioch, the problems came to a head. Paul was in deep trouble. Word got back to Jerusalem that Paul had been understating the values of Judaism, that he had been failing to tell the Gentiles the importance of Jesus's Jewish identity.

A similar message had got through to the churches of Galatia; new-Christian converts started to think that they had been short-sold, and that they could not be proper Christians unless they took on board the whole bag of Jewish law and tradition, including the essential badge of circumcision. The Letter to the Galatians is Paul's response. He has to face the typical conflict between the traditional and the experimental, the centre and the edge.

A community of churches which does not have a 'Jerusalem' element, valuing the long traditions of language and symbol which reach down into the subconscious level of the soul, will be an unbalanced representative of the Gospel. A community of churches which does not have a 'Galatia' element, claiming and consecrating new languages and new experiences of the Spirit, will be an unbalanced representation of the Gospel. And a community of churches which does not have an 'Antioch' element, providing a venue of encounter, confrontation, and mutual recognition, will also be an incomplete representation of the Gospel.

There were churches in Jerusalem, in Antioch, and in many other places around the Mediterranean. Even in Galatia, Paul is writing to 'churches', in the plural. Yes, there is a single church of God, the whole company of Christ's followers. But this is not a monolithic block. In its diversity, it can be flexible and creative, not always concentrating on those issues which its leadership can understand, but free to be led to discover new ways to touch the hearts of all. By the grace of God, we have churches, which have different stories and different songs, which can confuse and irritate each other, tell each other different stories, and somehow be held together, held together by the one feature that they have in common, the figure of Jesus Christ.

In South Africa, during the struggles against the ideology of apartheid when everything seemed to be going from bad to worse, we were occasionally blessed by visits from the church outside. One such visitor was a young Dutch theologian, Albert van den Heuvel. He joined our group of students one evening, and listened in silence to our sense of frustration and despair. After a couple of hours, he offered a few succinct responses. One of them, which has stuck with me as true in situation after situation, was simply: 'The Gospel of Jesus Christ does not come to abolish conflict but to convert conflict into tension.'

That is Galatians in a nutshell. But it is not a tension of equal strength on both sides. Our conventional church structures, with their cherished traditions and their reliance on structures of authority, their systems and covenants, are strong to affirm the value of communion and of stability. They do well to do so. But they have to recognise that the moments of new creation in our history have happened, not when someone has proclaimed the value of our tradition but when someone has questioned the boundaries, has bent the conventions of the law, has claimed the opening words of some of the oldest praises in our books, 'O sing to the Lord a *new* song!'[4]

Creativity does not spread out neatly in ripples from the edge to the centre; it often begins on the edge. And those in the centre, bishops and their sort, will be the last to hear of it. This is the classic pattern of Christian mission, starting with Jesus himself. Think what it would have been like if he had started in Jerusalem, had collected some nicely-turned-out graduates from an approved college, and had gone up to Galilee with a message, 'Good news for you peasants from headquarters.'

It might have indeed been good news, but it would have merely confirmed all the existing patterns of transmission and domination. Instead, he collects a hotch-potch of fishermen – you are never far from the smell of fish in the Gospels – along with bandits and dodgy collaborators with the occupying power; he moves from Galilee on the edge to Jerusalem in the centre; and the sophisticated citizens of Jerusalem recognise the provincial accent.

The Acts of the Apostles tells a similar story, of how our movement started from the obscure and troublesome province of Judaea on the edge of the Roman Empire, and moved towards the imperial centre. Before ever the church became an institution it was a movement; a movement is what it continues to be, to this day.

So we have Paul in a personal crisis. In the Letter to the Galatians, he is not just expounding a doctrine or laying down a moral code. He is telling his story, and his theology is in the story. The theology matters to him profoundly. As we listen to candidates for a national election, we can tell the difference between those who are in it for their own advantage, and those who just enjoy a political scrap, and those for whom the issues matter personally, who care passionately for the well-being of the people. In this Letter, more than anywhere else in his writings, we find Paul at his most personal, and his most passionate, and his most political.

The theology is happening in living situations. You can tell the real theologians, not by how many books they have read, not by how well they answer questions to which the questioner knows the answer, but by their ability to make a response of faith to a situation which has not been faced before. A truly theological church is always a New Testament church, where everything is happening for the first time. But that does not mean that it can happen only faraway on an undiscovered island. Every day and every place is something new, where the word can continue to become flesh.

So Paul writes to Galatia, sending greetings from his companions, his 'brothers'. We have a problem here, which modern translations into English have to struggle with. Paul wrote in Greek, where the word for 'brothers' – *adelphoi* – is so similar to the word for 'sisters' – *adelphai* – that the one word could be felt to include the other. In our Latin-based and German-based languages such as English, and in Celtic languages such as Welsh, and in British Sign Language, 'brother' and 'sister' are very different words; in recent years we have come to recognise that to use only the traditional male word has the effect of excluding female humanity, and fails to represent the inclusiveness of Paul's meaning.

So the translators of our New Revised Standard Version try various alternatives. Where they think that there is a strong stress on the close bond of 'brotherliness', they translate *adelphoi* as 'brothers and sisters'. But this is a clumsy and cumbersome phrase, so in other places they use the weaker word 'friends', or 'members of God's family'. Helpfully, the note in the margin tells us where the actual word is 'brothers'. Paul uses this word in addressing his readers at certain very specific moments, where he wants to emphasise the close relationship that Christ is making.

There is no single solution to this problem, certainly not in English language in its present condition. I would settle for 'brother-sisters'. Perhaps, in another generation, an inclusive slang term may have become acceptable, or even the sociologist's jargon-word 'sibling'. But for now we have to accept our communication-system with its strengths and weaknesses, and try to catch what Paul is seeking to convey. We are thankful for this ability to receive what has been written such a long time ago, The main meanings come out loud and clear, across the centuries and the continents.

For Paul, the figure of Jesus Christ is the one thing that matters, the one badge of the community. So, when some of his converts start to spread the notion that, in order to belong to the community, you have also to accept the laws and ceremonies of Judaism, he sees this as an attack on his authority, on the truth which is for him the most vital thing in the world. So he has to give an account of how he has come to have his place in the church, how he knows what he knows about the central fact of Christ. The ideas that the Galatians are finding attractive are not just an unfortunate mistake; they undermine his whole message. They mean that Christ is not enough, that the gospel of Christ has to be supplemented by obedience to the law, to a set of rules for which a person's obedience can be assessed and recorded, to a code by which a person can be judged as being either 'in' or 'out'.

Now, Paul is not attacking Jews. The problem is not with those Christians whose background is Jewish and who want to remain Jews; he is defending the right of those who are non-Jewish to remain non-Jewish. The problem is caused by Gentile Christians who want something more distinctive than the community of Christ. These good people find it difficult to live with true Christianity's carelessness about externals, who are unhappy with the apparently vague qualifications of our membership. Circumcision is a better badge than baptism – it makes a verifiable physical difference; and, for some, it has the advantage that the badge is carried only by males, and females belong in the community only as the attachments of males. Jewish Christianity was a precious element within the whole range of Christian membership; tragically, it largely died out; Gentile Christianity has lost its Jewish colleagues, and has yielded to the terrible sin which enabled the Holocaust. But we who are Gentiles would have betrayed something essential if we had allowed ourselves to be constrained by the Jewish identity. Jesus was a Jew, yes. But he belongs to all.

There is no one Christian language. When people come to feel that the language, or even the accent, derived from their parents is unsuitable for God, or when they are told not to use that language in daily contact, 'because it will keep you down', they are victims of a grievous form of cruelty. They are accepting a kind of slavery, against which Paul proclaims the freedom with which Christ has set us free. As the story of Pentecost shows, all the languages of the world can be claimed for the communication of the truth, and you do not have to be taken over like a ventriloquist's dummy in order to be holy.[5] The story of the Tower of Babel is interpreted by scholars in powerful cultures, such as English and

German, as a sign of God's punishment of human arrogance. But in minority languages, such as I have known among Welsh and Afrikaans-speaking colleagues, preachers have seen its message as a sign of God's deliverance from the threat of being dominated by a single imperial power.[6]

Paul is convinced that the Galatians can be Christians and still be thoroughly Galatian, and that they do not need to be remodelled into being pseudo-Jews. If Paul's policy had not prevailed, Gentile Christians would never have been able to feel that the church is *ours*. They would have remained, if they had remained at all, as second-class citizens of an alien movement – which is, of course, where many immigrant Christians and poor Christians feel that they are today, in the mainstream churches of Britain.

Wales is well-placed to understand these things. We acknowledge the leadership of the *cyfieithwyr*, the translators of the Bible, among them Bishop William Morgan, who worked at that task when he was vicar of Llanrhaeadr ym Mochnant. Through their work, its language has had an authority which has enabled it to survive the cruelties of the 'Welsh not' – a type of device which was also used in South African schools under the English administration, in an attempt to kill the Afrikaans language.

The Eisteddfod tradition has enabled Wales to make a precious gift to the rest of the world; this form of gathering has graciously provided the model for generating the International Eisteddfod at Llangollen; and this itself is a kind of modern Pentecost. There are many musical festivals which can be called international, insofar as they have people participating from across the world. Certainly, an event can be called 'international' if it offers, for instance, an English orchestra with a Welsh choir and soloists from the USA, Japan, and Bulgaria, singing works in German and Italian; that's fine, but I would call that cosmopolitan rather than international. The International Eisteddfod is Pentecostal because in it people are bringing their own languages, their own cultures, often representing quite small human communities, recognising and honouring the *mam-iaith*, the mother-tongue, of a great variety of people.

Christ is the new authority, coming to claim all our cultures. There may be elements in our culture which cannot be consecrated, which have to be opposed in obedience to Christ. But in due course, Christ as fulfiller will show what he can claim, and as critic he will show what he must displace. Our countryside has many places where sacred groves and wells have been taken over from paganism; they have been claimed and consecrated to Christ, and they remain as named blessings in the present day.[7]

But Christ also comes as critic and corrector; he comes to make peace where family groups have been in centuries-old conflict, and to correct the injustices in the claiming of wealth and land. Such influences of peace-making were God's gifts to our land, in the days which respectable academics call the Dark Ages, but which we call the Age of the Saints. Christ who is both consecrator and critic is the Christ who is new. We receive Christ, and add Christ to what we already know and have; and Christ the new will be master of the old.

That is the pattern of Christian mission which has been a blessing all over the world. But the danger represented by the Galatian situation is when people feel that Christ is the old thing and that Christ is not enough; we need additional disciplines to bring him up to date and to make us feel that *we* are 'in' and *they* are 'out'. That is, as Paul suggests, another gospel, a novelty which gives the feeling of being a 'gospel'. It is a gospel, because it is perceived a good news; it is not a gospel, because it divides member from member and leads away from the truth, away from Christ. And, typically, as we shall see in chapter 2 of the Letter, it is measured not by formulae or by creeds, but by the simple question, 'with whom are you prepared to eat?'

QUESTIONS

This is about Paul's story; what is your story? If you are asked, What is the most important thing for you in Christian faith, what would you answer? Why?

We notice three types of church:

- ❖ *Jerusalem*, where most people have belonged to the faith-community for a long time and are familiar with the tradition;
- ❖ *Galatia*, where most people are new converts;
- ❖ *Antioch*, the mixture.

What are the strengths and weaknesses of each?

Which is more like your church?

How often do you meet and compare notes with churches which are different from yours?

FOR THANKSGIVING AND PRAYER

Thank God for the Galatians, for that group of new Christians, young in faith, enthusiastic, open to new ideas, easily misled, without whose need there would no Letter for us to learn from.

Pray for today's new Christians, at home and across the world; that they may discern their calling and be faithful to Christ; that they may lead the rest of us into new learning, new obedience.

Pray for the people of the 'Galatian' area today, the people of Turkey, on the edge of Europe, working out their national understanding of Islam, living with the grievous history of the massacre of Armenians 100 years ago, in their difficult position on the borders with Syria and Iraq, with the claims made on them by refugees.

STEP 2

Climbing the first mountain: Mount Faith/*Moel Ffydd* Galatians 2:1–21

Paul's message in Galatians is clearly urgent. But the problems had not sprung up over night. At the beginning of his ministry, he had had a couple of weeks being briefed by Peter. Peter had himself recognised that the grace and truth of God were not limited to Jews; he recognised that Gentiles could be accepted and baptised into Christian membership; but he had never operated in a scene where Gentiles were in the majority.[8] But, evidently with Peter's approval, Paul moved off into genuine Gentile territory.

Paul says that he has been preaching and setting up church-fellowships among Gentile communities for fourteen years, and they have been developing on their own, on the edge, without interference from 'the centre'. But this was a temporary phase; Paul realised that he needed to make a move back towards the centre. The 'edge' church needs to be in relationship with the centre. But the centre-church also needs to know and be revitalised by what has been happening on the edge. Sometimes, in many different systems, great mistakes are made by administrative headquarters which are obvious to the humbler workers out in the field; and these mistakes are not necessarily due to stupidity or pig-headedness, but simply because the people at the centre have not been allowed to know what is going on. Management is at the mercy of those who decide what is to be told. Paul came to share his story, not to get approval or to forestall criticism, but simply to inform.

Circumcision now appears in the story, not as a matter of general speculation but concerning a specific individual. Paul goes to Jerusalem to meet the big men of the centre, and takes Titus with him. It would have been tactful if his travelling-companion could have been a circumcised person – it would have solved problems of where he could go and how far he could be admitted. But that would have meant that Titus would have had to give up being Gentile, as if Gentile-ness was something unacceptable. And Paul would not compromise. He would not allow circumcision to be given that kind of authority.

Our English words, at this point, do not quite convey the force of the matter. 'Circumcision' is the literal translation of the Greek, meaning 'cutting-around'. But our colourless negative word 'uncircumcision' does not convey the feeling of the word used in the Greek, which is literally, 'foreskin', a word of scorn and disgust. These 'foreskins' are second-class humans, the enemy, the unclean, they should not be allowed near decent society. For the Jews, the circumcised, they are the oppressing powers that have been grinding us into the dust for the last few centuries, who have been stealing our lands and humiliating us with taxation. That's what these 'foreskins' are about; and to allow ourselves to be dominated by them in religion as well as in everything else – well, that really is the end.

But Paul, Roman citizen and expert student of Judaism, is not moved by all this. His insistent conviction is that neither circumcision nor uncircumcision have any significance any longer, and neither do the status–differences of race or gender. This conviction was not based on theoretical analysis in a library, but by the implication of the question of whether one person, Titus, should have to undergo a very trivial form of surgery.

So six men met. Paul, accompanied by the uncircumcised Greek Gentile Titus and the thoroughly Hebrew Barnabas, came to meet James, Peter and John, the leaders of the Jerusalem church. The decisions of this little group were of fundamental importance. If they had gone down a different road, the Christian movement would not have survived and grown in the way that it has done. There would have been no community with the incentive to treasure and transmit the traditions concerning Jesus, his teaching and his activities. If any record had survived to this day, it would be merely an archaeological relic, not the witness of a living community.

The leaders in Jerusalem found no fault in what Paul told them. They agreed that Christians did not need the definitions and the badges which Judaism could give; their uncircumcised-ness made no difference. A new way of being community was being recognised, not by political engineering but by acknowledging a new thing that God was making; it was to be a community without insignia or qualifications. We are baptised, of course; but the water leaves no visible mark. Other groups, including Jews, can say how they identify each other. Christians can never be too sure. We are a uniquely ignorant people; we can be responsibly careless about this sort of question; and that is in itself a form of subversion to the world's conventions.

So much for the debate in the ecclesiastical headquarters. For us, its outcome has been of supreme importance. But, in Jerusalem, at the time, it would have passed unnoticed by the authorities. The meetings would not have been in the Temple, or in anything like an equivalent of Church House Westminster. The Jewish Christians were already in plenty of trouble with the Jewish authorities; and, if the meeting came in any way to the attention of the Roman authorities, it would for them have been yet another bit of in-fighting amongst the natives. The real test of the meeting happened elsewhere, in Antioch, the place of mixing and confusion.

But first, we should note the detail of practical implication of the ecclesiastical debate: 'Remember the poor'. Who were the poor, in this situation? Peter and his colleagues, the struggling left-behinds in Jerusalem, still there after many of their friends had been scattered as result of persecution by the religious authorities. The church in Jerusalem was both the source of all the story and the poor relation of the newer churches. So Paul agreed to remind the newer churches of their debt to the place of their faith's beginning. He was careful to fulfil this commitment.[9]

It was, indeed, a practical matter of money; the elements of the church which had financial advantage were called to make for equality with those who were poorer, to continue the leading of the Holy Spirit into sharing in a community of goods. But it goes beyond money. The meeting itself was a meeting of different levels of privilege; the ex-fishermen from Galilee had to engage with the cosmopolitan graduate from Tarsus, with his Roman citizenship and his well-travelled command of three languages. 'Remember the poor ' is a text which the literate, the well-schooled – the kind of people who get to reading stuff like this – should keep before them. How is your kind of religion going to be read by the poor majority of the world's people? They are the test by which our church activities are to be assessed; they represent the poor man of Nazareth.

'Remember the poor' is a text which all western Christians should keep in mind, as we look back to the place of our faith's beginnings, to the scattered, vulnerable people of the Holy Land, the Palestinians, the Christian minorities in Israel and Syria, the scarred victims of the holocaust; remember them as we remember Jesus. That remembering surely includes the dental clinic which the Church in Wales has been establishing in Gaza.[10] It is a kind of payment for what the Holy Land has given us. 'Remember the poor' should be inscribed at the bottom of every church agenda.

In his encyclical *Laudato Si,* Pope Francis has given his authority to the contention which bodies like Christian Aid have been urging for a long time, that a main reason for being concerned about climate change is that it bears most grievously upon the poorest. Our Anglican Archbishops in Britain, with their ecumenical colleagues, have been making the same call in their Lambeth Declaration of 2015.

Thirty years ago, church leaders in Oceania were drawing attention to the ways in which human exploitation was affecting the peoples of the islands of the Pacific. Now, the islands of Tuvalu are threatened with complete disappearance as result of rising sea levels. These islands are among the lowest carbon emitters in the world, but will be the first to suffer from climate change, according to the Archbishop of Polynesia, Dr Winston Halapua.[11] Climate change may mean quite a lot of inconvenience to the wealthiest of the world; it will mean total loss of home and livelihood to the poorest. The people of the Pacific Ocean are perhaps the least-heard voice in the world. Remember the poor, those close and those very far away.

We come back to Peter's story. When Peter visited Antioch, he had to move from debate about policy to face the issues in real life. At first, he was prepared to suppress his sense of Jewish identity; he ate with Gentiles. But then, people came from Jerusalem; he was scared of what they would say about him, and he withdrew from the table; his chair was empty.

If you are Peter, your behaviour is not a private matter. You quickly reach the boundaries of 'private morality'. Your actions are observed, and people may be offended. There are consciences other than your own which have to be considered. The need to protect the sensitivities of the people whom we know takes priority over the need to stand up for our solidarity with the people whom we don't know. Those who are under-privileged will judge those who are privileged by watching for the point where solidarity with the under-privileged becomes expendable. When push comes to shove, our community of race, or our community of culture, becomes more important to us than our community of grace.

This sort of problem cannot be solved by law. The law can knock away some of the obstacles that limit freedom, but in itself it cannot make us free. Any system which could make Peter's action illegal would be taking us back into the legalism which still had Peter partly in bondage. The law certainly has a role, and we need to use and cherish it as one of our Creator's gifts. As Martin Luther King observed, 'The law can't make you love me, but it can restrain you from lynching me – and that's pretty important also.' But then, as Dr King further noted, we need to be able to reach up ' to the majestic heights of the unenforceable.'[12]

When it comes to matters such as racism, there may be a very fine line between what can be achieved by law and what should be won by the education of conscience. The Church of England bishops offered a perceptive warning in their Pastoral Letter for the 2015 General Election, when they said that when law and regulation intrude too much into everyday life they create a 'chill factor' where anxiety about rules prevents people from acting freely and sensibly and with wisdom, even in areas which are not in fact governed by official regulations.

Further, the kind of problem faced by Paul cannot be solved by direct quotation from Jesus; indeed, that would be just another kind of law. Apart from the Gospel-writers, the New Testament authors say little about the teaching and activities of Jesus. They were in a different world facing issues which Jesus himself had not had to deal with. That should be encouragement to us, when we find that we cannot turn to Jesus and simply read off what we ought to do about nuclear weapons or zero-hours contracts.

We can certainly read the activities and the teaching of Jesus to find priorities for the style of God's kingdom; but, like Paul and the other apostles, we rely on Jesus's promise that his Spirit will lead us into truth – truth that is ahead of us, where we are first on the scene, where there isn't a prescribed agenda.[13]

It is typical of biblical experience that the trouble at Antioch was caused not by academic disagreement but by behaviour – in this case the most universal behaviour of eating. This is one of the very first conflicts in the history of the church – the first was about widows' pensions[14] – and it was about who should eat with whom. That is not to say that it was not a theological conflict. It was theological through and through. Peter's action was an example of heretical behaviour. Paul's reaction to it was not to tick him off for bad manners but to accuse him of betraying the fundamental meaning of our belief in Christ. Our task as church is not to be measured by our ability to get the liturgy right and the doctrine correct. Christianity is a matter of making the connections. A valid souvenir of the Antioch event would not be a statement of correct truth on paper; it would be a chair left cold by Peter and a piece of bread which he left uneaten.

Peter was right to be sensitive about 'what people will think'. His behaviour was scandalous, and he led his friends into the scandal. They were affected by his 'hypocrisy', by his assumption of a false role. His fear of offending old friends infected others around, so that the hypocrisy spread to all the Jewish Christians, including Barnabas, *even* Barnabas, who had been Paul's companion in their journeys into Gentile territory. Barnabas, the 'son of encouragement', is one of the most attractive characters in the Bible.[15] He was the kind of gentle, gracious person who could make Paul tolerable. Paul was not the nice guy. But sometimes the awkward uncompromising character may be right and the nice guy wrong. Barnabas-style people, on their own, may realise only too late that they have been more concerned to preserve their self-image of goodness than they have been committed to the calling of Christ.

Paul saw that Peter and Barnabas were wrong. They were wrong not in telling lies, or in breaking laws, but in failing to *walk* according to the truth of the Gospel. There is a word which is missing in our English language. We have a word 'orthodoxy', meaning the right way of expressing Christian truth in liturgy and worship. But we have not picked up the specific word which Paul uses here, 'orthopody', right-walking. This seems to be a word of Paul's own invention, a word to cover the practical implications of right belief. A faithful church would be a fellowship of 'orthopods'; if that sounds like a novel biological species, well, so be it!

Paul sees the behaviour of Peter and Barnabas and company as subversive of the Gospel, an improper innovation and deviation. When we insist that differences of race, or culture, or gender, or any other demarcation should not be allowed to break our community in the Gospel, we are being fundamentally conservative, standing for the church's most basic principles.

If all that Peter had done was just a violation of accepted morality, like putting a hatchet through Titus's skull, Paul could have dealt with it quietly, with a private rebuke. But Peter's refusal to eat with Gentiles was a crime of a quite different sort. It was a public repudiation of the Gospel. Peter could have been convinced by a quiet word in the corridor, but that would not have undone the damage. The offence has been in public; so Paul rebukes Peter in public.

Paul's rebuke is very specific. He does not attack the Jewish Christian leadership. He does not attack Jewish Christians in a Jewish area who continue to abide by Jewish law and tradition. He does not attack circumcision. He does not attack Peter as a person; he confronts Peter's behaviour in withdrawing from the common table. He recognises Peter's fundamental commitment, and appeals to him to be consistent and to realise the effect of his action. He is not undermining Peter's personal value; he is directing attention to the way in which Peter's behaviour would be seen and received by others.

This is a very precise example of responsible feedback, of genuine Christian critique, between colleagues and members of the family. 'Your action,' he is saying, ' in starting to eat with the Gentile colleagues and then in withdrawing from the table, is going to be seen by them as a sign that they cannot expect reliable fellowship with you unless they stop being Gentiles, adopt Jewish life-style, and cease to be an embarrassment to Jewish colleagues. Whose companionship is, in the end of the day, most important to you?'

And this leads to the central message of Paul's Letter, where his most personal, most passionate, and most political motives are poured out; it is the heart of the Letter, and of the Gospel. Elsewhere, we are given the story of the event of his conversion. Here he shares its real meaning. He is writing urgently, emotionally, and there are places where the interpretation is not entirely clear. I offer the following paraphrase, as an attempt to explore Paul's statement:

I agree that there are real advantages for those who belong to Jewish culture; we inherit a code of moral standards, and in comparison to us it is not unreasonable to call Gentiles 'sinners'. But we know better than anyone that the endless struggle to succeed in terms of verifiable standards and visible performance, keeping all the rules and regulations, does not give us true security; it brings only anxiety and competitiveness. That is what we Jews have been saved from, when we put our faith in Christ.

'But,' the objection will be made, 'if you people are so keen on your Christ that you throw overboard all the necessary distinctions, all the moral principles that lead to human dignity, are you not co-opting your Christ into a programme of degradation? Your idea of Christian freedom may be alright for people who are morally sophisticated, but these Gentiles aren't saints, they need a taste of discipline before they can be trusted. We must lift them up to our level, not allow ourselves to drop to theirs.' No; the old understanding had to go, and if I now start to rebuild it, this can mean only that I feel guilty about taking part in its abolition. And I do not feel guilty – the law itself tells us that it is not a sufficient guide and motivation. The law of Israel points away from itself to a time when people will live in commitment not to a system but to a person. It points to a future; that future is now present. There is now a new state of things, and we are given the opportunity either to accept or reject, either to welcome or to disapprove. This is a new society, a new way of being together in the world; it is not just an exchange of one set of rules for another.

In my journey to where I am now, I put everything I had into following our Jewish nation's traditions, the holy law. I obeyed it without compromise; I implemented it; I was its instrument, and its victim. It killed me. It left me with nothing that I could call 'me'. It allowed power only to the negative and destructive motives within me; it turned those energies not only against my fellow human beings but also against myself. But in dying by the law I found that I could still live even when the 'I' that had been a slave to the law had died. A new and real 'I' came into being, which could live without dependence on the law to give me identity, an 'I' which is created new by the God who is Lord of all people, those outside the law just as much as of those within. This new life is not my property to do what I like with, it is not a new instrument by which I can act to give me credit in competition with others. The dying which I have done is Christ's dying, his execution on a cross. He was killed by the systems of law, of prejudice, of exclusion, and he shares that dying with me. The life which I now live, a genuine life in this real world, is the life which he lives, because he showed himself to be stronger than the powers that *killed him, stronger than the powers which label us and separate us from each other and from God. The whole history of the Son of God, his living and loving and dying, have operated for me – **the Son of God who loved me and gave himself for me.** This is now the one thing that I know, that I am loved and that I do not have to show an achievement card in order to earn that love. Our group tradition, our law, could not convince me of that. It can give me some security in terms of my success, if I manage to do better than other people; but it cannot tell me that I am simply loved. I cannot go back on this conviction. If my place in God's favour comes because I deserve it through good performance, by getting a status or privilege over other people, then I am throwing Christ's gift back in his face; then I am saying to him, 'Jesus, your dying was a waste of time, and I don't believe that you are really risen and with me.'*

We have followed Paul through the thickets of his memories of his conversations with Peter and Barnabas. We have tried to keep pace with his struggle through the mire of his feelings about the law and about his personal formation as a Jew. Now, at last, he has reached the open air and clear light of his view on a mountain-top: ' The Son of God who loved me and gave himself for me.' He has arrived ; his view is not just for the confused people of Galatia, not just for his century. His message carries across the valleys and oceans and centuries. It is for us. He is sharing with us his discovery of Mount Faith.

'The Son of God who loved me and gave himself for me' is the strongest word of personal salvation. People who pride themselves on their concern for social and political issues sometimes despise this sort of emphasis, calling it pietism or individualism. But it is the root of political courage. Those who are truly secure in their sense of deep valuedness will have the nerve to confront the ideological idols which seek to claim our allegiance to policies of corruption and death. Systems of legalism and prejudice, of tyranny and exclusion, have an advantage. They can rely on our unlovedness. We all have been inadequately loved, at some stage, and we can be relied upon to behave accordingly. The law knows this; it can reassure us that we are not as guilty as some others. It can give that sort of security. As we see often in the activities of Jesus, law and custom can tell us what to avoid and whom to avoid; but they do not heal.

The love of Jesus can be the most important political energy in the world, not because it is a superior force that can crush opposition, not because it smoothes over the awkward issues and delivers a nice consensus, but because it releases us from depending on our own unlovedness and the unlovedness of others. The love of Jesus is permission to shout down the system; the love of Jesus enables you to stand up to your visiting archbishop in the presence of the whole congregation and point out that his or her behaviour is incompatible with the Gospel. If I reject, as Peter did, another Christian's fellowship, if I allow the community of race or culture to matter more to me than our community of grace, I am abandoning Christ's gift, I am abandoning my own true identity, I am abandoning Christ.

The voice that tells us that we are not loved can be very strong; it can be overwhelming. It shouts at us from the loudspeakers of systems which tell us that we are rubbish, that we are just problems, that we don't count. The apartheid ideology was an organised project to tell black people that they were inferior, that they had no place in proper society. For a black person, especially a black man in an urban setting, it was virtually impossible not to be a criminal. You were guilty of existing.

If you hear that message day in day out, it becomes difficult to disbelieve. It gives you incontrovertible reason for self-hatred; and you are licensed to hate the others who are similar to yourself. But you do not have to look six thousand miles away to find this sort of thing; only a few decades ago, the British law could tell you, if you were a homosexual male, that you were almost inevitably a criminal. Religion can do the same for you. It can tell you, by many devious devices, that you are fundamentally bad.

This is what Martin Luther found that he had to be delivered from, five hundred years ago. So he put this word, 'the Son of God who loved me', at the heart of his exposition of Galatians. 'Read therefore with great vehemency these words "ME" and "FOR ME", and so inwardly practice with thyself that thou with a sure faith mayest conceive and print this "ME" in thy heart, and apply it unto thyself, not doubting but that thou art of the number of those to whom this "ME" belongeth.'[16]

George Schofield was a priest who was very experienced in ministry with Deaf people in Britain in the twentieth century. At his regular Sunday service, conducted in British Sign Language, most of the congregation got thoroughly involved, as Deaf members usually do, much more than in the 'normal' hearing church. But among them there was a man who made no response, who just sat there like a bale of straw, totally uninvolved. George decided to try to engage with this man. He stopped in the middle of his sermon, managed to catch his eye, and then, with extra-emphatic signing, addressed him directly, as if he were the only person present, with the single phrase 'God loves you!' At this, the Deaf man sat stunned with delight and amazement; on the next Sunday, he nearly fell off his seat in anticipation. From then onward, George realised that at every service the man would expect and wait for a private sermon, a one-liner addressed personally to him.[17] Isn't that what should be happening for every preacher, and for every member of the congregation?

The love of God for us is the fundamentally energising fact of our life. It is at the heart of personal faith; it is also the mainspring of personal confidence, of defiance of all that the systems do in trying to control us. It's the religious equivalent of Don't let the buggers get you down. That is why this was the central message for that church in Sophiatown. And if we start to get tired of this same old story, if we come to feel that this is a rather dull message, that, if God does indeed love us without conditions or restrictions, and therefore there is nothing distinctive and special about us, nothing that makes us different from the general run of humanity, then we can take up the adventure of working out what it means that God loves our enemies and opponents with that same love.

And that puts me on the spot. I can identify my enemy only too well; Captain B of the South African Security police gave me a punishing time in a series of interrogations – although he was probably gentler with me than he was with his black victims. He and his boss, Major S, were, I am convinced, the primary actors in the process which led to me and our family being excluded from South Africa. It was the end of my ministry there and of all that I had been working for. The damage that they were doing, to us and to so many others, was profound. I cannot forget them. But if I allow my anger about this to dominate my feelings concerning them, I am allowing them to control me, to reduce my freedom. The love of Christ is as true for them as it is for me, whether they know it or not. But I do not forget. And what is to happen to my resentment and anger against them?

A remedy came to me very recently, a surprise and a blessing, in quite earthy terms (younger readers, please be patient with old gits like myself; for us, discussions about our geriatric failings and bodily fragility, in simple uncensored terms, are part of our way of life). Most old men have to get up a lot at night to empty their bladders. I, aged 88, am no exception. There is a positive side to this: I use a bottle, and then transfer my waste water onto compost, from where it goes onto the earth to nourish a row of beans. On this particular midnight occasion, as I let the waste water drain out of me, I was blessed with the sense that the old useless spiritual waste, of anger and resentment, was draining out of me at the same time. So the remedy is: let it drain! Perhaps useless old waste can transfer to a sort of compost of the spirit, to be recycled as a nutrient in readiness for new adventures – such as dying. Who can tell? As far as Captain B and Major S are concerned, I don't want to have any heavenly citizenship if they are not going to be citizens with me.

The love of Jesus is powerful in its meaning; but it is not a soft option for the rabble-rouser or the attention-seeker. Certainly, Peter's behaviour was disgraceful; but it happened under an immediate pressure for compromise. Powerful newspapers may delight to pillory such 'hypocrisy'; but under-privileged people often understand and forgive the clumsy, tactless privileged people who let them down from time to time. Peter is forgivable. The unforgivable would be a fake Paul. The love of Jesus is not about making stupid leaders squirm, or making bold confrontations, or claiming superiority in the love-business. If we claim to be truly loved, we share also Paul's claim, to have been crucified. If the love-claim, on its own, can be nothing more than euphoric froth, the claim of having been crucified, on its own, can be a paranoid bid for sympathy. Paul makes the two claims simultaneously, and both are linked to the love and the crucifixion of Christ.

Later, Paul has more to say about the meaning of Christ's crucifixion. But the first crucifixion that he speaks of in this Letter is his own, 'I have been crucified....' For Paul, a Roman citizen, crucifixion was not just a piece of conventional religious chatter; nor was the cross a conventional subject for religious art, gilded, hanging between candles. The cross was the instrument of judicial execution, the weapon of counter-revolutionary violence, the symbol of imperialistic reprisal against a disenfranchised people's struggle for freedom. Paul not only has the nerve to proclaim a liberator who is identified by this badge of subversion; he claims, first of all, that he, Paul, Roman citizen, has been crucified, has experienced the punishment which was administered to convicted terrorists. For a Roman citizen to claim that he has been crucified is the most dramatic way of distancing himself from the status of citizenship. For both the Roman citizen and the Jewish religious leader, crucifixion is the ultimate disgrace. The crucified one is an outlaw. Paul is following his master, downwards, alongside the most rejected and excluded of his fellow human beings.

So, crucifixions did not end with that of Jesus. In one sense, they started with him. Christ's disciples are not exempt from the destructiveness of the crucifying systems of the world. They share his experience of being victim, of being punished for refusal to let Caesar have the final word. But they know that, when they encounter the crucifying powers, they are not alone, that there is one who has mastered those powers and is alongside us. His victory on the cross does not release us from our involvement with the evil in our own real world, it brings us into closer encounter with it; it gives us a valid hope as we work out our own battles.

The conclusion of this argument is that the Gospel of Jesus Christ is not only a gospel of our human liberation but a gospel of the liberation of God. It tells us that God no longer assesses our performance in terms of a set of rules. At the Olympics, I feel most sympathy with the high-jumpers, the weight-lifters, and the pole-vaulters – their final attempts are always failures. They win because their failure comes at a higher level than anyone else's. With all due respect to their skills, they are models of the law, which gives credit to those who have not done as badly as everyone else. If this is our picture of God – and a lot of popular morality encourages it – our religion will be an expression of our anxiety about our place in the contest for moral approval. If our god is in business to preserve the categories derived from the past, we will wish to keep things as they are; change and forgiveness will seem to be unhelpful disturbances of good order. Anything which blurs the boundaries is dangerous, whether of race or culture or morality or class. This imprisons God; God is allowed to see only our origin, our guilt, our inferiority. By the Gospel of Jesus Christ, God is set free to see us as we might become, freed from the categories and adjectives by which we are defined. Those who worship God as the Father of our Lord Jesus Christ see our fellow-human beings as God sees them, through God's liberated eyes.

QUESTIONS

Are there events or contacts in your experience as a Christian which do not seem to fit in with the official system, which seem not quite 'normal'?

If you are in a group, break into three teams, one for Paul, one for Peter, one for Barnabas. Feel your way into your character; what is happening to you? Who is the problem for you? What is the solution? After a few minutes, let the three teams meet and share their experience.

How far can you go along with Paul's story? How far does it fit with your own story?

Take time to feel your way into Martin Luther's words; let them grasp you; make them your own.

FOR THANKSGIVING AND PRAYER

Give thanks for Antioch, 'the cradle of Christianity', where the new met the old, where Peter and Barnabas made mistakes, the point of departure for so much of the Christian mission.

Pray for today's mission agencies, where the experience of the new can be communicated to the older communities. That the old churches may still be generous in their support and their hope.

Pray for the Antioch area now; the Antioch of the Bible was in Syria, where the instability now seems almost beyond repair, where the Christian communities, some of them speaking the language of Jesus, are broken, scattered, and in grievous pain; where the centuries-old conflicts of the Crusades are still fresh in memory, and where the old economic wealth has vanished. The ruins of that Antioch lie across the border in Turkey, and the people of Antakya face the special challenge of being a border-community.

STEP 3

Thickets and brambles on the way to the next mountain
Galatians 3:1-25

'You mindless Galatians!' Back, downhill again. A precipitate descent from the high, universal, glorious truth of the crucified and risen Saviour, into the messy disorder of the people that Paul is trying to communicate with. You have let your minds be taken over by an irrational power. You have been fascinated, bewitched. How have you let this happen to you?

Sorcery: a power which takes over imagination and reasoning, an instrument of pernicious and deliberate evil. In Jewish culture, sorcery was a real danger. Sorcerers, in the Hebrew Scriptures, were foreign agents, subverting people's faith in the true spiritual authority of the one God. The sorcerers, the 'magoi' in the Acts of the Apostles, were the primal opponents of the Gospel, wanting to co-opt the energies of the Spirit into a self-centred acquisitive economy.[18] The magoi in Matthew's version of the story of the nativity of Jesus come to Jerusalem, not as kings but as the expert advisors and agents of kings, with their secret and manipulative interpretations of the stars, with political and economic aims of bending the new power to their own ends. They come with gifts suitable for buying alliance with a wealthy potentate; their project is turned into worship of the poor infant king of the universe. They surrender the wealth derived from their work, they hand over the tools of their trade. The powers of superstition have met their master.[19] But Paul sees that powers of this kind are still a threat; they have stolen the hearts of the Galatians. The conspiracy of evil has succeeded in displacing their response to the attractiveness of the true Gospel. This is not for want of correct information; the truth of the crucified has been placarded before their eyes.

Paul's mission has been a failure. But that has been a calculated risk. As a missionary, his task is to put the information before people, not to bribe or to brainwash them. He gives them the responsibility for making their response. He does not, like the sorcerer, play tricks with their eyes. His task is to ensure that if people accept Christ they accept Christ and not some caricature of him, and that if they reject Christ they reject Christ and not some caricature of him. This is the way in which Jesus himself communicated, in his parables. The parable was not a device for enforcing a truth with utmost clarity; it was a method for making people take responsibility for what they had heard. If they saw the point, if they could identify themselves with what was going on in the parable, good. If not, not. Anything else would be just another form of enslavement.

Nonetheless, as part of his liberating way of communicating, Paul can ask the Galatians to reflect on what has happened to them. What had made the difference, when they first became convinced about Christ? Was it the awareness of something which grasped them, made a new kind of sense, turned their lives around? Or was it a sense of achievement in obeying a new set of rules, of having made the right noises and pressed the right buttons? Is life for you a mechanism, a calculated way of fitting into a system of cause and effect, of work and payment, of stimulus and response? In that case, it does not much matter whether the currency you are dealing in is moral or religious or commercial or political; the effect on personality is all much the same. Or is life fundamentally a gift, a surprise, where you are content not to know the bottom line in advance, a freedom, even within the confines of an enclosing box?

Now, for us it is easy to see that the figure of Jesus well fits the second profile. But Paul is able to claim the figure of Abraham, as one who represents the second way of being a person, the way which Paul calls the way of faith; and yet Abraham is also the authority-figure for the system towards which the Galatians are so dangerously being attracted.

Abraham was the man of faith, going out not knowing where he was going, putting the future of his inheritance at risk in ignorance of the outcome. In his old age, he was in the care of the one who was ahead of him. Faith was not something which he possessed; it was his willingness not to possess.[20] His faith was made visible in his action, just as Peter's non-faith was made visible, not by means of some sort of super encephalograph monitor but by an uneaten piece of bread and a cold chair.

The story of Abraham is not a moral example, to encourage people to make an act of surrender so as to get God to be their friend. Abraham did not surrender to God because a preacher told him that if he did so God would love him and give him peace of mind. Nor was this a sign of despair or self-loathing. There is no trace of this sort of motive in the original story of Abraham, and the writers of the New Testament do not offer him as an example in that sort of sense, or as part of a conditional calculation. He is merely a model of what a person is like if they are simply sure of God's purpose and companionship.

Paul has to develop this argument in order to raise the key question, who are Abraham's descendants? The obvious answer is, those who can trace their ancestry back to him. That answer is fine for people who know themselves to be Jews. But it is of no help to the Gentile Galatians.

They are attracted by an alternative answer, that you are a descendant of Abraham if you undertake to fulfil the law of Moses. Paul's response to this is that keeping the law has nothing to do with being a descendant of Abraham. What made Abraham Abraham was not keeping the law – law of Moses or any other law – but faith. And that is the badge of the children of Abraham. But, unlike the other two answers, this is not another externally verifiable qualification. Paul does not say that you have to 'have faith in Jesus Christ', or sign up to a verbal creed. He does not speak of 'having' faith – possessing something which distinguishes you from those who don't possess it. He speaks of those who are 'out of faith', those whose starting-point is faith, those whose direction is determined by faith, those for whom faith is their base. Faith is not something picked up on the way as an extra skill: it is the propellant which moves you out on your course.

In all sorts of places and circumstances, irrespective of culture, race, or background, there are people who basically accept life as a gift, who are prepared to risk, who are open to the future, who go out content not to know everything in advance, who are willing to live without guarantees. Those people are the children of Abraham, because what was most true about him is what is most true about them. God had told Abraham that in him all groups of people would find their blessing. And it is people of this kind of faith who see, almost instinctively, that the gospel of Jesus makes sense. What in the past had been a general sense of freedom and openness now has been portrayed in the figure of one person. The story of that person's life tells of an infectious way of spreading a defiant inclusive care for other people; the story of that person's death tells how the systems of the world, and the powers of evil, find that this sort of faith is an intolerable disruption of our customary stability; the story of that person's resurrection tells that faith is stronger than despair and that life is stronger than death. And that 'faith' can claim the commitment, not only of the rather privileged few whose background has already helped them to be free spirits, but also of numberless nobodies whose background has told them that they are not worth bothering about at all.

The downside of all this is that the opposite kind of people are under a curse. This is not a curse upon people simply on account of the fact that they obey the law – the law of Moses or any other law. Paul calls them 'those who are out of works of law'. They are people whose starting-point is working according to a system or rule, whose direction is determined by the power of a rule, those for whom a rule-system is their basis of life. Paul is thinking, in the first instance, of those who commit themselves to a rigorous obedience to the law of Moses, who judge themselves and who judge other people by their success or failure in keeping such law.

But there are other kinds of legalism to which Paul's judgement would apply just as critically. Paul is primarily thinking of those who, from outside the law of Moses, find that tradition something to envy. People who are born and brought up within a culture like Judaism may well keep that law happily and freely because it is part of their back ground and comes naturally; that would be true of the Christians of Jerusalem. But people who look at such a culture from outside, and start to insist on keeping the law in all its detail show that they have found a system to surrender to, their motivations will be more specifically directed to establishing themselves in a slave-state; and they will find themselves engaging in a competitive score-card in evaluating themselves against other people. They will be unlikely to discover the joyful freedom which is possible for those to whom the law is a natural environment.

For people of faith can be found living and thriving within cultures which, from outside, look rigid and systematic. Monks and orthodox Jews can be more relaxed and free than some who boast of being liberated. Poets and musicians may discover the same about engineers and lawyers. The real difference has little to do with cultural background and occupation. To grasp the difference at all, we have to beware of all stereotypes, for they trap our perceptions into another malign system of law.

The curse is not a noise being made by an angry god; it is simply the opposite of blessing. It identifies that here is something which obstructs the free movement of the grace of God. The law is a curse if it makes obedience to God a matter of achievement, of establishing ourselves as successful in the competition to be good. The Gospel of Jesus Christ saves us from the demand to be good. This is not because goodness is no longer good, but because the effort to be good is essentially self-regarding. The law is a curse, because, although it is a good thing in itself, and offers a good ideal, it draws us to evaluate ourselves in terms of our own performance, and causes us to see the other person as either more successful or less successful than ourselves. Law then becomes valued as a device for detecting other people's faults and giving us a lever for making other people feel guilty. Guilty people can be held, tricked and manipulated; this plays into the hands of those who wish to retain the controls and to keep other people servile. The curse is, therefore, not a punishment; it is simply a fact.

Paul was a dangerous man because he was not guilty. His arm could not be twisted; he could not be manipulated by many of the usual human fears. He was no longer a slave to his own need for approval. He no longer had to be good in order to feel assured of God's love. Christ was not a new resource to make him better than he would otherwise be, or to enable him to excel in the moral competition against other good people. Christ had put all that kind of question into the past. Paul knew that he was not guilty, not because he had never incurred guilt, not because he had suppressed his awareness of guilt, but because he knew that he had been declared not guilty by the one who had the authority to do so, and had been released by an undeserved acquittal. He was free from the curse. A community of people who were equally convinced of their acquittal would be the most subversive force in the world. They would defy most of the usual definitions and distinctions; they would be impossible to manipulate or predict. And that is what the Christian community is supposed to be.

Does this mean that we are free from the curse? That would be the logical and welcome outcome. But Christ's work takes us deeper; Christ took us out of the market-system (the literal meaning of the word translated as 'redeemed') of the law by becoming a curse for us. The manner of his death is most evidently and obviously a curse. The biggest challenge to the first Christian communities was, how can you expect us to take you seriously when it is obvious that your so-called saviour was judicially condemned to death by the best law of Judaism and the best law of Rome? How can you defend yourselves against the accusation that you are supporting the claims of a religious charlatan and a political terrorist?

Paul, in his earlier life, would have been able to make maximum capital of this blindingly simple proof of the Christians' ethical and political worthlessness. But the Christians refused to soften their outrageous stand. They acknowledged that the Saviour whom they proclaimed had died as one who was guilty and cursed. As the crucified, he was associated with everyone condemned by the systems of law. And there was no glory in this; in Judaea, crucifixions happened three at a time. In his death, Jesus joined all those who have left life under a curse. Especially in Jewish sensitivities, part of the curse of crucifixion was that (despite the traditional loincloth in the visual arts) the crucified criminal was stripped naked, with 'nothing to bless himself with', no covering, no disguise, no insignia. There is nothing superstitious or magical in saying that a person who is hanged is cursed; it is a simple statement of fact.

As a follower of Jesus, Dietrich Bonhoeffer was cursed as a traitor by his country's leadership, and was hanged under Hitler's authority on April 9th 1945. Years before, he had spelled out some of the implication of Christ's calling. He reminded us that in Christ God had come to be our brother; 'God will not be separated from our brother; he wants no honour for himself so long as his brother is dishonoured.'[21] That is a caution that should be inscribed upon every worship-book of the Christians, upon the agenda of every liturgical commission.

The first Christian preachers did nothing to conceal the dishonour of their Master. Indeed, it was a vital part of their message that Christ had shared and carried the burden of the guilty; he had been treated as rubbish, alongside all whom law and custom treated as rubbish. He was innocent of sin, yes; but that was not because he had passed the morality examinations with a higher mark than anyone else but because he had not allowed himself to be bent away from his total commitment to the will of God. His innocence did not isolate him from sinners but put him into the same bag with sinners. A private innocence can only emphasise the distance from the guilty; Christ asserted his solidarity with the guilty. A total private innocence could be achieved only by being isolated from the real world; Jesus belonged in the real world, with all its ambiguities and compromises.

This is the kind of Christ, the kind of Messiah, that Jesus provides. He demonstrates that our hope does not lie in moving away from evil, either by pretending that evil doesn't exist or by establishing a private innocence whereby the best performers in the morality-contest get the highest marks. Christ, according to the Christian Gospel, means a liberation from that whole way of being oneself and of regarding other people.

The Christian message is that the one who had thus been 100% rejected by religious and political law, 'whom you crucified', had been recognised by God as Lord and Christ; and therefore our whole normal understanding of morality and justice and goodness was subverted, cancelled, and shown to be rotten.[22] He has come through to the far side of the processes which killed him, and he is alongside those of his followers who share his exposure to the cruelty and flawed judgements of the best of human institutions.

In calling and baptising us, he invites us not to discover a pristine innocence but to accompany him into the environment of the curse. He invites us to share in the mastery which he has himself discovered in our own world of cruelty and confusion. That is our hope, not an optimism which says that it will be alright in the end, but a hope that what we are doing is worth doing, even if, and perhaps especially if, it means being cursed. Now that, surely, is pretty formidable theology. How often have you heard a preacher deliver an invitation to join a leader into the experience of being cursed? Yet Paul, addressing new Christians who are attracted by various soft options, pulls out all the stops and entrusts them with some of the most off-putting aspects of the Gospel message.

All this is bringing the blessing of Abraham to the Gentiles; those who have hitherto been privileged are bringing the knowledge of God to the outsiders. But it is not a one-way traffic. The response of those who were receiving the Gospel is bringing completely new gifts to those who are doing the evangelising. Because the outsiders are receiving the blessing of Abraham, we (Paul himself, and the other Christians, Jews and Gentiles alike) are receiving the promise of the Spirit. They are, in a new way, living in terms of promise and gift rather than in terms of bargains and rewards and moral economics. Involvement with the new is enabling the old to discover how to live by grace. This is not because there is something unusually good about the Gentile outsiders but because of the nature of the energies released by the sharing of the Gospel.

But Paul feels that there is more to be said. He gnaws away at the problem of the law. After all, the law of Moses was at the heart of his own formation; he cannot lightly set it aside as if it no longer meant anything to him. Further, it was the law of Moses which had grabbed the imaginations of the Galatians as a most desirable aim, and which threatened to steer them away from the truth that is in Christ. So he points out two features of the law, which put the law into its place.

Firstly, it is incorrect to say that the law came first and then the promise. God is promise-maker before he is law-giver. Promise is the beginning and end of our being human. Promise is both caterpillar and butterfly; law is only the chrysalis. Law is a temporary, adolescent phase in the relationship between God and ourselves. In that phase of life, in Paul's culture there was a functionary called a paidagogos – translated as 'tutor', or 'supervisor' or 'disciplinarian'. Such a functionary can be found in any society where there is a great gap in privilege between one section and another. This paidagogos was a slave, to whom the privileged parents would hand over the responsibility for the upbringing of their sons, preparing them for a life of privilege which he himself would never share. He was a functionary within an educational system by which society reproduced itself. Paul also speaks of the law as a gaoler. For both these functions, he sees Christ as liberator. An educational organisation may be genuinely intended as enabling, liberating, and fulfilling. But a structure which the powerful feel to be free and flexible may be experienced by the less privileged as merely a more flexible kind of tyranny, a system against which you can never win. The close connexion which Paul can make between law as educator and law as gaoler should make us wary.

There is a well-observed moment in the film of 'The Englishman who went up a hill ...' The Englishman was measuring the hill on behalf of the Ordnance Survey, to check the accuracy of the maps. For him, the purpose of the map is obvious and benign, to help people to find their way around. The minister of the Welsh Chapel is not so sure. The map is going to be used to define property. It is to serve the *Ordnance* system, the system that controls by weaponry and domination. It is to be a tool of the powerful, an instrument for enabling control. It is a device of the London-based law. *Byddwch yn ofalus!* Beware!

When the time of faith comes, Paul says, the role of the paidagogos falls away. Faith, even in a young person, is maturity; it is a willingness to receive life as gift, to see God as the one who gives more than necessary for survival, who takes us way beyond our deserving. If we take law as the superior, permanent basis of life, we see other people, and we see ourselves, in terms of our comparative deserving. The valuable people are those who do best in the morality competition, and get through the various filters by which our culture selects people for privilege. We become better at making comparisons than we are at receiving gifts, and our religion becomes a means for satisfying our competitiveness. Our keenest skill is the skill of detection where people are on the status-ladder.

It is not correct, either, to say that the Old Testament is about law and the New Testament is about Gospel. The Old Testament begins with Gospel, the good news of the promise to Abraham that the human race will be blessed through him. In God's dealings with Abraham, God established his character as promise-maker and giver. The same God is our creator in the New Testament. God does not wait for the law to be obeyed. God has blessed us by being born among us when the law was most thoroughly not being obeyed. The land was ruled by a cruel paganism, the official guardians of the law were mostly isolating themselves from the common people in a secluded religious establishment; the real keepers of the law were a few elderly nobodies and a teenage girl. And there the promise was being fulfilled. Blessedness is God's nature and God's generosity, and no system of selection can override this or organise it. Some may count themselves as blessed because they are physically descended from Abraham; others because they are successful in keeping a set of rules; but the character of God as giver and as promise-maker cannot be pinned down by any such formulae.

They were stripping old wallpaper in an ancient farmhouse, when they found a vertical line marked from top to bottom on a wall. It showed the names and, in some cases the dates, of the heads of the family that had lived there through the centuries – *Emlyn ap Iorwerth ap Morus ap Ioan ap Elfed ap Gruffudd ap ...*, and, near the bottom a little note: 'at about this time, it is believed that the creation of the world took place'.

In our part of the world, we are very interested in our genealogies.[23] We don't often read aloud in church the genealogies of Jesus in Matthew and Luke; they are important, because they show that Jesus was not a rootless world-citizen; he belonged, as each of us belongs, in a flow of human lineage.[24] So we say that Jesus was a Jew; but that does not explain Jesus; it does not tell us why not all Jews were Jesus. Any scheme of things which tells us that the most important thing about us is that we are someone's descendants is part of the conspiracy against Christ. We may be in a system which tells us that our national or racial identity is supremely important; we have seen, in the twentieth century, most obviously in Germany and South Africa, the disastrous effects of such idolatry, of such insistence that we need a more exclusive identify to give us security. Gwenallt, an outstanding Welsh poet of the 20th century, must have had this hazard in mind when he had his vision of St David, the national icon and patron saint of Wales:

> ... *A soniodd ef wrthym am Drefn naturiol Duw,*
> *Y person, y teulu, y genedl a'r gymdeithas o genhedloedd,*
> *A'r Groes yn ein cadw rhag troi un ohonynt yn dduw.*

> ... he talked to us about God's natural order,
> The person, the family, the nation and the community of nations,
> And the Cross preventing us from turning any one of them into a god.[25]

Another system may tell us that our place in the world is determined by our parents' education or social status or economic value or by their claim to outright possession of land – land which, in the law of Moses, belongs to the community as a whole, as the property of God. But if I come to believe that I am what I am primarily because of something which I automatically inherit from my forebears, I am rejecting my identity as a child of promise; I am insisting on devaluing my own humanity.

Secondly, law exists as a response to evil. It is a modification of the original design. It is intended to control or counteract evil activity. It is valuable, therefore, as a device or tool or mechanism for achieving certain purposes. But those who take law as their fundamental way of life or basic identity are condemning themselves to a bondage to gloom; they are basing their security on the persistence and reliability of evil. In Christ, evil has met its master, and law has only a limited usefulness. A life based on law may look realistic; in fact, it is the way of despair. Murphy's law says that if something can go wrong it will. David Niven said of his fellow-actor Errol Flynn that you can absolutely rely on him to let you down.[26] Realistic; but, in the end, fatal.

Our imprisonment by law makes us unable to be simply good. Our checklist of the rules requires that we do not merely have to be good, but good enough to compensate for yesterday's badness. So we settle for a lower standard, so that we may get a surplus. Our goodness is not done for the sale of goodness, but so that we may be able to balance our virtue-account. Each good action is a reminder that we have accepted a lower standard than we should. To compensate for our inferiority, we pay higher and higher prices, making greater and greater sacrifices. We may be able to recognise this in ourselves; but as a society we may see the same mechanism spreading out to involve more and more people in this general frustration. We know that we *must* do what we *cannot* do. We may persuade ourselves that we are succeeding, by trapping more and more people into a system of benevolent cruelty. Their suffering will convince us that we are trying hard. More and more people become used as the raw material out of which we try to organise our security. Vulnerable minorities and depressed majorities become imprisoned in restrictive systems, while the powerful swap their anxieties with each other about the latest form of the crisis.

When we live by faith, accepting the word of promise, we can give up this urgent interest in being good; our security no longer depends on that sort of success. This frees our own spirituality; it also frees us from the demand to co-opt other people into the spiritual economics of our own search for acceptability. We are no longer under the supervision of a paidogogos, an enslaved disciplinarian who will check our behaviour and see that we fulfil our obligations; we are adult children of the household. We are not bound by contracts or assessed in terms of productivity.

There is no real *purpose* in being a child or having a child. Faith operates to remove calculations and purposes. It enables us to stand where we are and just to be, without needing to or being obliged to. According to our Gospel story, the curious condition of our human nature is that this precious unnecessariness is such a difficult thing for us to grasp that it required the whole mechanism of Good Friday and Easter to bring it within range.

Earnest preachers and radical prophets may batter our ears by demanding that we attend to 'what the church should be doing'. Certainly, there is an urgent mandate for us to seek the Kingdom of God and his justice; at the same time, we do not justify ourselves by our usefulness – to God, or the civic society, or anyone else. We celebrate our unnecessariness in the style of our worship and fellowship. We are not wrong to be concerned about relevance and effectiveness; but we are, first of all, members of the family, an outpost of purposeless being-for-its-own-sake.

QUESTIONS

Are you interested in your ancestors? How far back can your trace them? How much does this matter to you?

What is your nationality? What does this matter to you? Do you have close friendship with someone of a different nationality? What nationality would you regard as enemy? Do you know any Christians of that nation?

Are you a good person? How do you know? How do you judge? Is there someone whom you feel is not as good as you, or someone whom you feel is better than you? How do you judge?

FOR THANKSGIVING AND PRAYER

Give thanks for Jerusalem, for all that it means, for Jew, for Christian, for Muslim; for its ancient role as a meeting-place, for its survival after so much destruction, for its place at the centre of the Gospel narrative, the place of cross and resurrection, the place of Jesus's prayer; for its meaning as a symbol of the hope for eternity, the haven and the home for all.

Pray Psalm 122, for the peace of Jerusalem; for Israeli and Palestinian, their leadership, their citizens; for justice in the occupation of land, and for the removal of the Wall and all that it stands for; for the Christian churches, in their diminished numbers and their dividedness.

For our old-established churches in our own day and place; for our continuing task of the treasuring of the traditions of holiness; for the right testing and receiving of new witness and new hope.

STEP 4

The view from Mount Unity/*Moel Undod*
Galatians 3:26 – 4:7

Paul has led us again through the thickets of his own reasoning, about the purpose of the law and his own place within it. Now, again, at last, he reaches the clear open air of the summit; he has the view from the top of a new mountain. This is Mount Unity. The view extends way beyond Galatia and its local hassles, demanding though they may be. This is for the world. This is for us. There is no longer Jew or Greek, there is no longer slave or free, there is no longer male and female; for all of you are one in Christ Jesus. The differences between human beings are no longer more significant than our common humanity; they can no longer insist on their own power to tell us who we are or where we belong or whom we must exclude.

The problem for us is not in our differences or our distinctivenesses, but in how we use them. Marvellously, humans exist in a wide variety; we could line up a long row of people from across society, standing alongside each other, and never exhaust all the possibilities of variation. The trouble comes when we convert this horizontal spectrum of difference into a vertical ladder of status. Then we are no longer asking the simple question, 'what sort of person is that?' We are asking, 'is that person above me or below me in the system?' The other person ceases to exist in their own right, and becomes important to me in telling me where I am placed. I will have to get the other person's identity and classification as clear as I can; I will establish those features in which the other person most clearly differs from me, and I will establish my own identity in the same way. I will value those features which most clearly make me distinguishable

At first sight, Paul's statement is nice and kindly and uncontroversial. But every one of his categories involves not just a balanced pair of differences but a clear distinction of status. A Jew is superior to Gentile, a free person is superior to a slave, a male is superior to a female. In each case, the distinction is valued as a means for deciding who should have power and who should not. From his earliest years, Paul would have been taught to thank God that he was not a Gentile or a slave or a woman. So, at this point, he is not merely commending a general truth; he is renouncing his own upbringing and culture; he is rejecting his own place on the status-ladder, and the mechanisms that have placed him there. And he is making this statement, not just because of his philosophical reflection or speculation but because of something that had happened to him that had turned his own sense of his identity inside-out.

The features which are most significant in establishing these distinctions are all based in the past. The difference between Jew and Greek is not really a difference of race, in our modern sense; but it is a powerful difference of culture and inheritance. We are not wrong if we extend Paul's category to apply it to racism as we know it today. In a racist society, the past decides our classification, tells us our value, allocates our place in society. Our parentage decides how acceptable our language or accent will be, and will tell us who of our fellow-humans we should beware of. The determinisms of the past are more important than any possibilities of change in the future. Change is a threat, not an opportunity.

It is no accident that a racist society is likely to be also an unforgiving society. Those who are afraid of change attach much importance to sin, sin being anything which can disturb the clarity of our classifications. If a person has offended, that fact becomes an indelible part of their identity; forgiveness would confuse that identity and therefore is not to be encouraged. The problem of racism is not caused by our awareness of racial difference, but by our political assumptions which enable racism to thrive. Racial difference can be used to justify the distinctions of status; that was abundantly clear in the structures of South Africa during the apartheid regime, which deprived black people of their inheritance in the land[27] – the Sophiatown process was just one example of a nation-wide programme of land-thefts. Remove some of the rulings which enforce racial consciousness, and the result is that a few members of the oppressed group can be absorbed into a status-system devised for the benefit of the oppressors. During the apartheid years, there were black people who were profoundly conscious of this possibility; their warnings were not given the attention that they deserved, and the land remains unshared.

So, 'unity' is a fine ideal, a splendid goal. But always the question has to be faced, unity on whose terms? The apartheid system was developed when South Africa was part of the British Empire, when it was entitled the 'Union of South Africa', established under an Act of Union, in the time of King Edward VII. When you see the word 'Union' used in this way, look to see who is being cheated. What about a certain Act of Union under King Henry VIII, passed to bring 'unity' by disallowing Welsh language and legal tradition? As they used to say in South Africa, what is the cash value of a reconciliation between a mouse and the elephant that is treading on it? It's necessary to be realistic, when we talk about peace and reconciliation. If you wish for peace, don't go and talk about peace with your friends; you have to go and talk with your enemy. And when Paul spells out the categories of Jew and Gentile and so on, he is not talking in a generalised way about universal categories. He is talking about real live Jews and Gentiles, slaves and free people, males and females, in the Galatian churches, people who will have to come to terms with each other or else the whole Christian enterprise will be wrecked. That was true in Paul's day. The categories may change, but the problems of status remain.

In Paul's day, it was the Jerusalem church which set the norms, and it was the Gentile church which provided the problems and misfits. But within a hundred years, the church of the circumcised had started to disappear, and even the Jerusalem church had Greek bishops. The 'normal' church became the Gentile church of Greek and Latin speakers; before long, they would be singing such un-Hebrew songs as the Nicene Creed.

The first disciples, and Jesus himself, the circumcised Jew, and his mother Mary, would be strangers and misfits in our modern western churches; it was, I think the story goes, in a church school where they chose a popular girl to play the part of Blessed Mary in a Nativity Play, but then discovered that she was Jewish, and therefore disqualified her for the role. This ancient disunity is not high on the agenda of most churches, but it will not go away. The fulfilment of 'unity' has to keep pace with social change, and there will always be new hazards on the way, new people to bear the cost of being excluded.

In Christ, in the baptised community, the divisions of status are done away. Where, as in Paul's lists, these divisions of status come in pairs, it is important that there should be a genuinely new commitment for both components. Part of Paul's concern was that the Gentile Christians were being attracted by the culture of the Jewish Christians; but if they took on board the apparatus of Judaism they would never be more than second-class citizens in that community, in the same way that a few honorary blacks found their way into a scene dominated by whites, or a few honorary women were assimilated into a scene dominated by men. The persons might change a little, but the pattern of domination would remain as before.

In South Africa as we knew it, politics consisted of white people arguing with white people about black people. In this country, we have bishops, who are mainly elderly white heterosexuals, without a single declared homosexual among them, and we have for years been debating the rules for homosexual people. It is not inappropriate to extend Paul's categories to include the distinction between 'gay' and 'straight', for this is another discrimination on the basis of a person's unchosen nature. It is no accident that, in its new constitution, South Africa has set itself against discrimination on the basis of sexual orientation. Further north in Africa, this may be regarded as evidence that South Africa has become too westernised and has been infected by an alien decadence. But there is a sense in which black South Africans are the blackest of Africans, in that they, more than any other Africans, have been structurally and legally penalised on account of their blackness.

If you have got involved in the struggle against one form of prejudice and exclusion, you will find yourself logically drawn into the struggle against other forms; neither oppression nor freedom is limited by such boundaries. So, as we rightly value the unity of, for instance, the Anglican Communion, or of the Church of England, it is also right to ask, on whose terms? Whose interests, whose opportunities, are set aside as we seek and cherish this unity? Is this the unity for which Jesus has prayed, the unity which he creates? Raise your hand if you are a gay priest who has stood alongside your life-partner in public, saying 'I take you ...', and then found some, shall we say, difficulties in being taken on board by the church's appointment systems.

There is another scene which rightly fits into Paul's categories, in which people are divided into those who are 'in' and those who are 'out' on account of their unchosen features, namely disability, The structures of society, of support, of employment, and of access, are still largely devised for and by the non-disabled – even though most of us should reckon ourselves as being only temporarily non-disabled! The councils and committees which are concerned with disability are still largely organised by the non-disabled.[28] The demand 'Nothing about us without us' fits very appropriately into Paul's vision. Here again, we remember that Paul's vision is not only about the justice of the Creator; it is about the meaning of Christ. It is 'in Christ' that the divisions are overcome.

It may be difficult to reconcile our experience of disability with the concept of a Creator-God of supreme perfection. But the 'Christ' identity takes us back to the person of Jesus himself. In Jesus, people can and do find a model of humanity which bridges the divisions of sex and race and culture. The Gospel is that there is one Christ, one only for all. Jesus was a Jewish male; he is known to us largely through the writings of Jewish males. But they stress his capacity to defy this kind of categorisation. In the Gospel story, his role and activities are defined not by his sex or culture-group, but by his freedom and passion for the truth about God and humanity. In his lifetime, he was more completely human than his culture could tolerate. And so non-Jews and non-males can find in him our model and our pattern.

You do not have to resemble Jesus in order to do his work; you do not have to be a young Aramaic-speaking carpenter's son, with a Jewish accent and circumcised genitals, to represent his word, his mission, and his sacrifice. But he did know excludedness. He seems to have had an instinctive understanding of sign-language and lip-reading; he was blindfolded, was silent, was tied and immobilised, was treated as rubbish and laughed at and done to death outside the city. For those who cannot hear, he is known as the word made flesh, who is known in action and touch as well as in speech. For those who cannot see, he is the image of a God who is beyond light and darkness. For the scarred and excluded, he is the God who is among us eternally damaged, bearing the scars of his experience in the heavens, who has known our excludedness and has mastered it, who calls his followers to be his body, to embody all these features of his incarnation. He was not a wheelchair user, any more than he was an African, or a Roman Gentile, or a female; but women, and Gentiles, and LGBT people and Deaf and blind people, people with disabilities and learning difficulties, elderly people, dying people, as well as black people and European people, have been able to recognise Jesus as 'one of us', as 'on our side'.[29] This is part of what it means to be 'in Christ'. When this is true for us, we are nerved to stand out against the disorder of a society which gives privilege to a part and withholds it from the whole.

In Christ, Paul claims, even the economic division between slave and free was done away. Was it? Many centuries had to pass before anything approaching the reality of this vision was recognised structurally, and there is still a long way to go. The enfranchising of both slaves and women in the early church did not happen completely, and Christian writers like Paul are today accused of being too accommodating to the status quo. But, alone among the writers of antiquity, the apostolic teachers addressed both slaves and women as responsible moral agents, able to make decisions and to take care of their own consciences; the principle was beginning to take effect. The hassles and confusions in the church of Corinth could not have happened if slaves and slave-owners, civilised Greeks and barbarian peasants, traditional Jews and sophisticated Gentiles, powerful men and angry women, had not been trying to be one church together, one community of the disciples of Jesus sharing one communion.

In our day, these groups would probably have been meeting in separate conventicles, each finding a church which suited them. Especially in the big cities, you can easily go round and find a church which suits you, which makes least possible demand on you to change, so that you run no risk of being converted. And if you find a church which suits you, the chances are that you have found a god who suits you. The theological term for a god who suits you is an idol.

Paul's language slightly shifts when he comes to his third pair of categories. There is, he says, no longer such a thing as male *and* female. This is not a matter of 'male *or* female?' It is a different kind of question. It is the dilemma of two beings who are deigned to be a unity, but who in their very co-existence represent the most basic kind of hostility. The 'and' represents a division which is all the more painful because it can also represent unity. The work of Christ is not just a matter of patching up the tensions within the Galatian church. Christ is overcoming a basic hostility in the heart of humankind. Nothing is a more efficient conveyer of the infection of evil from generation to generation than the hostility between parents. It is from our experiences with them that many of our motivations are built into us, such as the motivations which make us so concerned about our place and status that we feel compelled to insist on the 'Jew-or-Greek', 'slave-or-free', disabled-or-non-disabled' kind of question.

We use the gift of sexual identity to restrict our gift of power. Power, the mandate to be responsible for the rest of creation, is a gift to the whole of humanity, and if we limit it to a subsection of humanity we forfeit our hold on it. Our culture reserves overt power to males; males are 'normal'; females have special facilities, special sections in the supermarket; they are not 'normal'. The healing of our disordered understanding of sexual identity is part of the salvation of the whole humanity, and it is not achieved yet. Those whose sexual identity does not conform to the norm may see themselves, with good reason, as victims of an oppressive culture. But the subtle switch of the question from the polarisation of 'male or female' to the inclusivity of 'male-and-female' may be a sign that the abnormal can aid us towards a renewed normality.

Paul himself was not outside the categories that he was discussing. He evidently did not succeed in consistently applying the practical implications of his deep perception, when he came to give advice about the place of women in church or society, for instance. But it is easy to be consistent when your fundamental perceptions are conventional. Two bishops under whom I have served, who were in a profound and costly way committed to human liberation from oppression, could often be authoritarian, rigid, and inflexible. But, if this was inconsistency, I would prefer to have it so, rather than lose the leadership in vision and inspiration. Paul's perceptions at this point were as radical and unconventional as any in the history of thought or politics; they derive directly from his conviction of the meaning of Christ. Better to have the vision with inconsistencies than to have consistency without the vision.

We recognise these distinctions of status when we identify the 'problems' of society. 'We employ domestic servants so that we have time to go and drink coffee with other employers and discuss the failings of our servants.' For Jews, the Gentiles were a 'problem'. Women are a 'problem'. So are claimants, people on benefits, people growing up on corporation housing estates, 'the disabled', gays, pedestrians, the third world – you name it. If they are seen to be a problem, they are taught that they are a problem. But if we belong together in the eyes of God, in Christ, the problem can shift. The poor are not our problem, we are the problem for the poor. So, we do not ask how we can give to the poor but how we can stop taking from the poor – how can we stop making the poor poor? The education system and the social services may tell a child that she is a 'problem'; the Church, the Body of Christ, can tell that child that she is valued, that she has personal status in the eyes of God; it can tell her that she has got something to offer, and can make it real.

Paul has stated that we share in this participation in the character of Christ through baptism. Is he affirming the abolition of barriers and classifications, just to establish another? Is not baptism just another ritual, a new kind of insignia, a badge of membership of just another in-group? Does not this new identification create an 'in-or-out' situation, just as specific as the 'Jew-or-Greek' demand?

But baptism has to be seen as a fulfilment of the work of Christ, a way of applying the principle established in Paul's statement that in Christ the distinctions are done away. Baptism, if it is insignia at all, is the insignia of those who renounce insignia. As with Christianity itself, the importance of baptism is its unimportance. It is a strange tool, with an edge which cuts at those who try to use it as a tool to cut others. A person who is baptised is committed to the dethroning of all the idols which cause exclusive in-groups to form. Compared with religious and cultural initiation ceremonies old and new, baptism is the most absurdly simple event. Of secret formulae, arcane passwords, complicated rituals and elaborate paraphernalia there is no end. The Gospel's simple secret is that you join God by getting wet.

But is this for real? Father Trevor Huddleston told the story of a discussion which he had with a young Afrikaans-speaking van-driver who was delivering meat-pies to the Priory in Sophiatown. They were debating the rights and wrongs of the apartheid system and the separation of the races. The van-driver summed it up with the remark, 'Our difference is eschatological.' Father Huddleston commented, 'How many Anglican van-drivers, speaking in a foreign language, could have used that term so accurately?'[30] It was indeed accurately used. The Afrikaans-language churches, on the whole, subscribed to the teaching that the true church is invisible, known only to God and existing in heaven; the doing-away of the categories of Jew and Gentile, free and slave, male and female, is true in the purpose of God and in the work of Christ, but its truth is of the invisible church, under God's own sovereign authority which he does not share with any human institution; it is 'eschatological', for the time of the last things, for the world of the future, and so it does not provide a mandate for the ordering of the affairs of this world. Well, this is a creed with a worthy starting-point, designed to restrain the excessive claims of the earthly institutional church. The danger is that it enables us to tolerate the continuance of dividedness which Paul claims is no longer true. And this is convenient for those who are satisfied with the status quo, and who do not want the grace of God to disturb it. For them, the present arrangements, the laws and structures, work well.

About 300 years after Paul, a teacher arose within Christendom, a British monk called Pelagius. He gave rise to a whole school of thought which was named after him. It is difficult to discover the actual teaching of Pelagius; he certainly offered good counsel about prayer and personal morality, and some straight condemnation of the great inequalities of wealth and poverty which he saw around him. But Pelagianism became a movement which caused much concern among the church leadership; it taught that we can be pleasing to God by our own human efforts, by strong self-discipline, by keeping the precepts of the law of Christ, and by trusting our God-given power of reason to choose between good and evil. This could produce a community of the 'real Christians', superior to the common crowd, refusing to tolerate sin in oneself or others. The Pelagians acknowledged that we may not be able to save ourselves; but we are able to live a sinless life and obey the commandments, and therefore sin is neither inevitable nor excusable. This kind of teaching met with considerable success; it was attractive to those who were secure, confident in their moral and intellectual strength, and who were looking for a way of life that could stand firm amid the chaos of the collapsing Roman empire. But, in the eyes of the orthodox church leaders, it was dangerous, because it gave so little value to the special work of Christ and the gift of God's grace. In terms of Paul's message to the Galatians, it was a return to the attractions of living by law. It depends on getting a sense of success in achievement, in competition for status. And so it becomes a new form of slavery.

Pelagianism was attractive to the Christians in Britain, so much so that a highly-respected bishop was sent here to preach and to teach in opposition. This was St Germanus, bishop of Auxerre, in central France. His mission was well received; he was so popular and effective that churches in many ancient sites are dedicated in his name in the Isle of Man, in

Ireland and England, and especially in Wales; you meet him wherever there is a place named Llanarmon. Apart from all the sermons and formal statements made by church-leaders against Pelagianism, I think that the most perceptive insight comes from the twentieth-century Welsh politician and playwright, Saunders Lewis. He wrote a play for radio about St Germanus, entitled *Buchedd Garmon* – the Life of Germanus – and he put the following statement into the mouth of his hero:

> *Canys arnom ni*
> *Disgynnodd dydd yr amddiffyn,*
> *Dydd y ddeublyg amddiffyn,*
> *Dydd adeiladu'r Gristnogaeth a chadw'r ffin.*
> *A pha fodd y gwarchedwir y ddinas,*
> *Pa gyfannedd a wnawn,*
> *Pa gydadeiladu mewn cariad a pha gydwylio*
> *Onid ydym yn un yn Adda, yn un yng Nghrist?*
> *A hyn yw drwg y Pelagiaid,*
> *Chwalu undod ein natur, a'n hundod newydd drwy ras,*
> *Fel na bo gŵr llên yn un genedl â gŵr tlawd,*
> *Eithr ennill, ohono ei hun, ei nefoedd ei hun*
> *Mewn hunan-foddhad diysgog*
> *Yn nydd goresgyniad y Goth* [31]

Saunders Lewis himself gives the literal translation:

> For upon us has descended
> The day of defence,
> The day of dual defence,
> The day of building Christianity and of keeping the border.
> How can we guard the city,
> what communality can we achieve,
> What building together in love and what guarding together,
> If we be not one in Adam and one in Christ?
> And this is the harm the Pelagians do,
> They break the unity that we have in nature and our new
> unity through grace,
> So that the scholar is not of one nation with the peasant,
> But acquires by his own effort his own heaven
> In unshakeable self-satisfaction
> On the day of the triumph of the Goth [32]

The play was written in 1937, at the time of terrible economic slump. Saunders Lewis was an academic on the staff of what is now the University of Swansea. As he explained: 'In Swansea and in Merthyr I had for some three years been working with the unemployed and had got University College Swansea to cooperate in arranging extension lectures for the young out-of-work, But the majority of teachers in the Welsh University were little concerned.... The whole of this passage refers to them, the *gwŷr llên*, which in modern Welsh means the writers and scholars. They also, while the out-of-work were rotting in hopeless hell, were very placidly enjoying their scholarly security. The Pelagian heresiarchs made, as I thought, a fair comparison. The play throughout is a contemporary document.' So the scholar, the privileged literate secure achiever, is able to disconnect from the poor peasant, refusing the claims both of natural humanity and of the grace in Christ which unites us. And, we might add, there may well be a peasant within the scholar which may be yearning for recognition, and there may well be a scholar inside the peasant whose voice is unheard.

This exactly fits Paul's message that the grace of Christ overcomes the disunity of our status and performance. But if we maintain disunity within the church on earth, we shall expect and desire that that same disunity should be maintained into the invisible church of heaven. The grace of God is rejected.

Eighty years on, and our social conventions still celebrate our disunity. Our media function as a device to congratulate celebrities on being celebrities. Our academic world serves to congratulate the clever on being clever. An established church functions as a device for congratulating the powerful on being powerful. The sports world congratulates physically successful people on being physically successful. An advertising world congratulates beautiful people on being beautiful. Exclusive churches serve as devices to congratulate morally good people on being morally good. Consciously or unconsciously, they all depend on there being others who fail. The Gospel of Jesus Christ speaks to the nobodies, the stupid, the disabled, the ugly, the morally compromised, and says to them, 'Congratulations to YOU; you are made in the image of God, and God sees a reflection of himself when he sees you; Christ is your brother, who loves you and has given himself for you. You are valuable, whatever anyone else may say. There is a place for you; you belong; and you do not have to achieve anything to prove it.' That is the heart of Paul's message to the Galatians. It is the heart of the Church's witness in every age. And it should be the battle-cry of all churches dedicated in the name of Saint Germanus.

Charles Jenkinson was vicar of one of the poorest parishes of Leeds at the same time as Saunders Lewis was teaching in Swansea. He also became leader of the Leeds Labour Party and Chairman of Leeds City Council Housing Department, in charge of one of the biggest slum-clearance programmes in Europe. At one of the many public meetings which he addressed in order to explain the programme, a gentleman stood up and said, 'I quite understand that you must provide new housing for these poor people, but why are you sending them to live near me in Moortown?' Jenkinson answered with another question: 'Who the devil are you? And who the devil am I? And who the devil is anyone to say "My fellowman is not to live where I live"?' (The opposition press went to town on this slightly unclerical language.) He went on to justify his stance by quoting Paul's doctrine of baptism – 'I, as a priest of the Catholic Church, am bound to admit to the Family of God, with the same baptismal service, the child of a prince, of a prostitute, or of a drunkard.' The same form, the same meaning, the same value. And the same value is expressed at every Eucharist: the body of Christ, given for YOU – the same meaning, the same value. In the Body of Christ, it is made visible; it is not left to the other side of death. In Christ, we belong together.

A noble, uplifting vision. But it has to be made true. Jenkinson got involved with slum-clearance and housing reform precisely because he felt that he could not go on baptising infants if he was not doing something about the rats which threatened the survival of so many children born in his parish[33] Or, as Canon Henry Scott Holland of St Paul's affirmed, at a time when cholera was rife in London: 'The more I believe in the Incarnation, the more I care about drains.'

'All one in Christ.' It is easy enough to sing that excellent hymn, 'In Christ there is no east or west'. But to be true it has to be local. When I was appointed as Rector of a parish in Zululand, I found, in a single churchyard area, a fine stone church, designed by a top-flight British architect, behind it a new hall, built of brick and glass, behind it another church, made of corrugated iron held together by cobwebs, and behind it a low shack. The stone church was the church of the white people, who were also the owners of the hall; the iron structure was the church of the Zulu people, and the shack was the house of the African curate. For my installation service, which had to be in the 'white' church, I suggested that the African people be invited to join the white congregation. The Zulu churchwarden, a fine man, a police sergeant who became a good friend, said 'We have never been welcome in that church before; why should we come along now, just because you say so?' In the end, he did come, and the point was made. But normally there were two churches, two congregations of people who lived next door to each other in the town, but who never met. The government interrupted this convention, by decreeing that the African people should no longer be allowed to live in the odd shacks and rooms in the gardens of the white town; a new township was built for them, three miles away, with better accommodation than they were used to. They liked these new facilities, but they knew full well that the fundamental reason for the move was that they were considered 'surplus natives', not wanted in the white town. And it took only a couple of hours for their old church to be demolished, and forgotten. Separate churches, separate heavens; Saunders Lewis's picture spelled out exactly.

All over Wales, there are towns and villages which have separate churches for Welsh-speakers and English-speakers, or at least there are separate congregations using one building. For other activities during the week, members of the two groups meet and work and play together; but for worship they are apart. As Martin Luther King observed, 'Sunday is the most segregated day of the week.'[34] How is the community of the village offered to God, in worship and commitment? How are the people of God nourished for a ministry to the people, the village, the environment? And when the authorities decide that one church has to be closed, which is the loser? When I was a bishop in Shropshire, I sometimes said that there should be a 'Bishop of Shrewsbury's Law', that you could have as many churches in a town as you liked, provided that you did not have two. A market town might have a fine historic church, expensive to maintain but attractive for weddings, and a newer one, built for 'the poor'. Two parishes, with the boundary cutting right through the middle of the town, obstructing attempts at coherent mission to the whole community. And when there was any talk of redundancy, it would be the church for 'the poor' which would get the chop. 'All one in Christ.' These are not easy issues to sort out; bishops and parish clergy and congregations have been wrestling with them for years, and there are some fruitful solutions. But this is where Practice Interpretation bites, when we try to hear Paul's message to the Galatians.

Are there people in your church who you would prefer not to be there? Are there people who make you feel awkward, people you would prefer not to associate with, people with whom you could never agree, people whom you could never really trust, people who stand for things which you could never accept? If not, why not? Is it that your church is so keen on being reckoned as 'friendly' that it keeps some people out? Does it, consciously or unconsciously, set up standards that everyone agrees on? Perhaps it is keen to say, 'All Welcome'; but does it mean it? It is possible to have a vision or an ideal of 'community' which is the enemy of real community, that we would prefer to the real people that are next door to us; as I have suggested, there is a dangerous level of 'choice' in town areas; we can go round a lot of different churches until we find a church which 'suits' us. There aren't so many options in the countryside, either you put up with what there is or you give up. The churches that Paul was writing to were bundles of misfits. They belonged together not because they liked each other or agreed with each other but because the Gospel message had brought them together in spite of their differences – Jew and Gentile, slave and free, male and female. This was the reality, and it was in danger, and they needed all Paul's persuasiveness for them to hold together. So, as he advised the church in another city, they should accept each other, not because they liked each other or agreed with each other, but because Christ accepted them.[35] Christ was not in business to fulfil their fantasy of what community should be like, but to show that, in Christ, peace had happened.

This is, perhaps, most difficult for the 'professional' Christians, the ministers. We would not be ministers at all if we did not have some vision of what the church should be, and anyone who disappoints that vision is a block on our hopes. In my experience, one of the most demanding and rewarding parts of a bishop's work is in the choosing and appointing of ministers to local churches. These ministers then find themselves licensed by the bishop, to work with other ministers as colleagues in local neighbourhoods; their acceptance of each other, in spite of differences of style and background and outlook, is part of their obedience to the bishop. Sometimes we get faithful ministers who are anything but obedient in this particular respect! We develop our theological skills in order to become accusers of each other rather than colleagues. And it all becomes part of the competitive, achievement-centred discrediting of Christ that Paul is trying to cure. 'He who loves his dream of a community more than the Christian community itself becomes a destroyer of the latter, even though his personal intentions may be ever so honest and earnest and sacrificial.'[36]

But all this is danger to beware of. The positive truth is that in Christ each of us is a gift to the other, not by our choice but by Christ's. We belong with each other in a way that cannot be undone. The unity across our human divisions is a reality made by our Creator; it overcomes our separateness at the same time as it affirms our distinctiveness. The unity which we have in Christ is the reality. We can affirm it or we can deny it or; we can celebrate it or we can begrudge it; we can reveal it or we can conceal it; we cannot create it and we cannot destroy it, because it is not our construction but the creation of the Eternal.

QUESTIONS

Consider the questions toward the end of the previous page. How far does your church represent the whole community in which it is set? Is it really inclusive? Would you prefer it if some kinds of people were not there?

Have you found a church which really suits you? Are you still looking for one?

How could your local church be better organised so as to include people of different languages, people with different kinds of disability? What sorts of people are made to feel that they are not welcome?

What changes would be needed if this nation were to be truly One Nation?

FOR THANKSGIVING AND PRAYER

Give thanks for our own nation, for its history, its landscape, for all that has made it what it is. For the transmission of the truth of the Gospel over the centuries, so that it has reached us in our day. For our place in the international fellowship of Christian communities; for our links with the faith of our ancestors, and with the faith of our colleagues in Christian discipleship across the world.

Pray for the leaders of our nations, especially in the UK and in Europe, as there is so much exploration of our distinctiveness as nations and of our need for each other in the pursuit of all that makes for peace. And for the leaders of our churches, as we live with ancient structures and as we seek new ways of being signs of the Kingdom of God in the present day.

STEP 5

More problems on the road, swamps and sidetracks, with some merciful signposts
Galatians 4:8–31

With his great proclamation of the doing-away of barriers and categori-
sations, Paul has reached his second summit, Mount Unity. Now he
descends to a confusing area of wandering pathways and bogland; it is
the area of slavery.

Slavery is a system, in which a person has no value except as a functionary, a producer. In it, one group of people has the power to decide
the value to be placed on another. The slave is the victim of the market;
redemption – the Greek word might literally be translated as 'de-mar-
keting' – happens when a person is removed from this market and from
this kind of valuation. It abolishes the right of the powerful to decide
the value of the less powerful. It abolishes the boundary between slave
and non-slave. The slave ceases to be a slave; and in due course slavery
itself disappears. That is the theory, the vision. Christian faith began to
achieve this, when, in the New Testament times, slaves started to become members of the church, along with slave-owners. Politicians and
lawyers, and writers who to this day are counted among the world's
greatest-ever philosophers, defended slavery as a necessary fact of life.
Athens's celebrated democracy would have been impossible if its citizens
had not been served by a huge army of slaves.

But apostolic writers addressed slaves, as no one had ever done before,
as responsible moral agents. Slaves were being addressed because they
had a voice, they were able to command attention. In the church to
which Paul was writing, they could cause trouble; the nobodies could
teach the somebodies, and still remain in the one church. The church
provided an environment within which the disparity of power, as recognised in secular terms, could be overcome, and the somebodies could
see that this was possible to live with.

This was true within the Diocese of Zululand as I knew it, during the
apartheid era; there were far more black people than white people in the
parishes, and therefore black people had greater voting-power in the
Synod than white; but, within the business of the church, white people
realised that, although this was totally contrary to what law and culture

required, it was not impossible. The church, in spite of its weakness and its mired-ness in compromise, could still be a sign of a different world.

The battle for the abolition of slavery is far from finished, even within so-called Christian cultures, and there are nearly 30 million slaves in the world, more now than ever before. The UK Government has passed its Modern Slavery Act, because of the need to protect people from slavery even within this country. In our liturgies, we give thanks that we are delivered from the slavery of sin, but the meaning of this is betrayed if we are not seeking, for all people, deliverance from the sin of slavery.

Paul tussles between three kinds of non-freedom: there is the non-freedom of being a slave; but this is, in effect, the same as the non-freedom of being an immature minor and the non-freedom of being steered by irrational superstition. Paul has already suggested that the problem for the Galatians is that they have been bewitched – their minds, their reasoning, their decision-making, have been taken over by irrational dominating powers. We have already noted some of the implications of the surrender of the powers of superstition in Matthew's story of the journey of the magoi. In my experience, this story has been received with joy by rural Africans, precisely because it tells of the supremacy of the poor Son of God over the domination of the powers of darkness, whether these be operating through traditional 'witchcraft' or through contemporary systems of dominance which deny people's value and responsibility.

'Witchcraft' is a word to denote a great bundle of forces which can control the human spirit, unseen, arbitrary forces which determine one's health and fortune, forces which can be understood by an in-group of specialists who have access to secret language and arcane manipulations; against them, one doesn't stand a chance. There may be many forms of witchcraft oppressing us today, in science, in the media, in the intricacies of computer technology. But the most pervasive, the most widely-felt, is surely what is referred to as 'the market'. This well fits what Paul calls the 'ruling spirits' of the world. In the past, he says, you Galatians were ruled by them. They were the powers of paganism – just as the recognition of the supreme power of 'the market' is a form of paganism. Now, in your eagerness to submit yourselves to the laws of Moses, you are returning to paganism – 'an extraordinary proposition to come from a Jew who in earlier years had surpassed all his contemporaries in enthusiasm for the ancestral religion.'[37] For you, this would be to make yourselves slaves. You are handing yourselves over to a system of rules and regulations; you are rejecting the Gospel's invitation to live as explorers, without boundaries; the attraction of circumcision is the attraction of handing back your freedom; you are going to allow yourselves to be ruled by the mindlessness of the calendar.

All right, we may, in the Christian order, have our commemorations. But we do not see history as primarily a wearisome repetition of commemorations. Christ has come into history at a midpoint. If we have commemorations in our calendar, it is to celebrate the Christ who is being born in us *today*, in his Body, and who is risen *today*, in his Body. At every celebration of Christmas and Easter, there should always be some element which is new, something which is unexpected. In the sign-language of Deaf people, the normal gesture for 'the past' is, naturally enough, a pointing behind oneself, and for 'the future' a pointing forward. But there are some Deaf people who do it the other way around; we point in front of us to the past, because we can see it, and to the future behind us, because we can't see it.[38] We are like rowers in a boat; we are progressing towards a destination which we cannot see – but of course we are steered by the coxswain, who can!

A slave has a place in a household by fulfilling certain functions. A child of the household is there by right. In these days, we claim that our place in society should not be determined entirely by our parentage or ancestry. So, we identify ourselves by what we do rather than by what we are. It is more important to be a nurse or a management consultant than to be a black person or a Scot. Good. But we are most able to exercise our function within society if our basic identity is secured in a status which does not depend totally on our performance. Just to shift from a class-based society to an achievement-based society may be nothing more than a shift from one form of slavery to another. The meritocracy says that our value is reckoned in terms of what we can produce; and that in turn is demonstrated by what we possess and how much we consume. A society which gives us value by enabling us to travel more and more air-miles is hardly good news for our grandchildren.

Our achievement-based society makes freedom possible for the healthy, the non-disabled, the competent, the successful; it segregates the unsuccessful, the incompetent, the disabled, the misfit, and allows them less place than they can have in less 'successful' cultures. It makes failure very difficult to cope with. In order that there should be a satisfactory number of people who feel successful, there must be a minority of failures. In some areas, it is predictable that some people will be failures even before they start going to school. They are condemned to a kind of enslavement. But those who are in bondage to a success-image are also enslaved. Failure, for them, is disaster. And death is an offence which ought to be reckoned with only when it is absolutely unavoidable.

There are lots of jobs to be done in the church – more now, perhaps, than ever before. Our ministry is spread out more and more widely, and

more and more people are involved in its functioning. And that is good.
We need our churches to be successful; we need our members to take
their share of the work and to do it well. But a slave – and a slave-church
– can't afford to fail. And sometimes our calling is to get into situations
where we are almost bound to fail. If a thing is worth doing it's worth
doing badly – not an appropriate motive for architects or heart-surgeons,
but it may sometimes be a right motive for apprentice-saints. A slave-
church will get impressive results by stressing the need for its members
to improve their performance, get good training, and meet targets. It
will give status to the members who are a credit to it, and quietly side-
line the misfits and the un-clever. It will concentrate on activities for
which it can claim success; but if it is too keen on avoiding failure, it
will fail to be the one thing that it is designed to be, a community of the
children of God, members of God's household. The members of the
body need each other. 'Not only do the weak need the strong; the strong
cannot exist without the weak. The elimination of the weak is the death
of fellowship.'[39]

Paul, Roman citizen and graduate of the best Jewish religious education, knows only too well what slavery is like and what liberation is like.
He has known God as, in Milton's words, the Great Taskmaster. And
he has come to know God in a quite different mode. He has known
redemption, being taken out of the market where one's value is reckoned in terms of one's achievement. And he yearns for the Galatians to
claim this redemption. Among the people to whom he writes, there are
some who are slaves. And there are some who are free. The message to
both is the same: not just that you are free, but you have the freedom of
being members of the family. You are brothers and sisters together. In
this family, those who are members of natural families, with the privilege
of being treated as children of the household because of their birth, and
particularly those who claim Abraham as their natural ancestor, have no
advantage; their membership of this new family is not by virtue of their
natural ancestry, but because of their adoption.

Paul introduces this notion of 'adoption' without explanation or elab-
oration. Adoption is a beautiful word, a word of gift, generosity, and
grace. It offers remedy for parentlessness and childlessness. It is faith,
hope, and love in practice. It is about compassion, loving choice, patience, struggle, disappointments, inclusion, and, above all, potential. It
is a precise window into the character and purposes of God; and there
are examples all around us, of people who have given and received in
this procedure. Moses, exposed to death as a tiny baby, adopted into
Pharaoh's household, goes on to become, in spite of his incompetence
as a public speaker, the leader and liberator and law-giver for the people
of Israel.[40] Nearer home, John Rowlands, illegitimate and abandoned,

absconds from St Asaph Workhouse, is adopted in the USA in the name of Henry Morton Stanley, travels deep into unknown Central Africa to deliver his immortal one-liner, 'Dr Livingstone, I presume', and ends up as an English MP with a burial in Westminster Abbey.[41]

Our adoption in Christ gives an inheritance and a membership far beyond that of our natural ancestry. We are sisters and brothers of Jesus Son of Mary, Jesus, whose last act before his death was to create a new family, giving his mother to be mother of his best friend and giving his best friend to be son to his mother.[42] The genealogies of Jesus in the Gospels are lists of his male ancestors; they are part of the story and have their place. I, and millions like me, owe our surnames to that same tradition, which says that male ancestry tells us who we are. But, in spite of the genealogies, Jesus is known as Son of Mary. The unique title 'Son of Mary' dethrones the traditional power of male naming. It recognises the relationship in which human structuring primarily takes place, the work for which the remuneration of the minimum wage is ignored in the calculations of politics and economics and educational design, the role for which the church deigns to dedicate one Sunday out of 52 each year. Hail Mary, full of grace....

Paul says that God sent his Son, born of a woman, born under law; strictly, he says not 'born under *the* Law' – the Law of Moses – but simply 'under law'. To be born of a woman is the universal human condition; to be born under law is also universal, because everyone is born under some sort of organisation or authority or system of culture. Christ comes to share the human condition of being under law, so that he can 'de-market' those under law. Certainly, his redemption is for those under the Law of Moses, that is what the argument with the Galatians is about; but that is only a small part of what 'the law' means. Redemption is about delivery from the power of structures of violence, economic domination, superstition, cultural exploitation, exclusion, of systems which keep the poor poor, the rejected rejected, the homeless homeless. It is about the implementation of the Lord's Jubilee, as delineated in the Law of Moses and in the preaching of Jesus. The promise of such redemption is still very far from being fulfilled; but the promise is part of our belonging, true for Jew and Gentile alike. Our adoption is into the new community in which all human inheritances and cultures can belong and be healed.

According to Paul, God is one who sends; God is, therefore, outside us. God is not where we are; God is distant and other. This is not a fashionable kind of language in these days. We have learned to cherish the picture of an intimate God, who is closer to us than breathing. Certainly, the notion of a remote God who is way out of reach, high above the highest human – and therefore most accessible to the highest-placed humans in the pecking-orders of religion and state – is much more congenial to tyrants and dominant powers than the message of Jesus would allow. It is no bad thing that our prayers to 'Almighty' God are being balanced by prayers to 'Generous' God, 'Patient' God, and God who suffers with us. But the God of the Scriptures is still the God who is outside, able to criticise, judge, interfere, and send.

We need to bear in mind that, even in our most physical organisation, we are not self-sufficient and independent; we are subject to the most basic elementary fact, that all our energy on earth is derived from a source which is outside us, separate from us, namely the sun. Our theology, too, needs to be bold to affirm our dependence on that which is outside, beyond our control; our careful efforts to make God intelligible will be like using a kitchen-knife to dig a coal-mine. If we lose our sense of God's beyond-ness, we starve ourselves of our source of energy for renewal and growth. At the same time as our religion has been embarrassed about its message of a distant God, and has been keen to offer a domestic God, in our physical organisation we have become most thoughtless about our use of non-renewable resources. If we fail to proclaim our alien God of righteousness, who stands over the world as critic and deliverer, we will in effect be supporting the systems of exploitation and oppression, which disadvantage the world's poorest and make nonsense of our cosy language about all being one family.

This God decides. God is the master of God's timetable, of God's interventions, God's delays, God's interpretation of history. God sends when this is right. God is not manipulated by mindless calendars or by the movements of stars or by human systems of calculation. 'When the fullness of time had come ...', had come by God's choosing. A period of adolescence had been completed; it was time for a new stage. The Son is sent, not when the world has become good enough to deserve his presence as a reward, not to celebrate a victory won, but when conditions had developed to the point where his arrival would precipitate the sharpest crisis. God remains the master of his timetable; his servants might prefer to be left in a less demanding state, to stay perpetual teenagers. We may look back on adolescence as a time when life was simpler, when success came without so many complications. The arrival of Christianity does seem to have created more problems than it has solved; it has brought crises and dangers which the world did not know before. A faithful local church may well have to face some such experience; and so may the Christian who grows in discipleship.

The Son is the one whom the sending God has sent. The Son's work is to make us a family of adoptive children, with one Father; the Spirit of the Son makes us able to use the Son's language and to call this God 'Abba, Father'. That is the language of the child who is no longer a minor, who has grown up, for whom father is no longer tyrant or owner or gaoler or enemy or rival or censor. This kind of maturity cannot be organised or legislated; it cannot be purchased in the market-place or earned by acting as a slave. It does not come automatically by the passing of a birthday. It happens; and according to the Christian Gospel it happens because God sent the Son into the world, and the Son has discovered and revealed what genuine sonship is like and therefore what true fatherhood is like. The best evidence of this is in the seventeenth chapter of St John's Gospel, where we overhear the Son's conversation with the Father. It is like hearing one side of a telephone conversation; by hearing the speaker whom you can see you can get a picture of the person on the other end of the line whom you cannot see. The Father sends the Son, for a purpose, and the Son achieves that purpose. But this achievement is not done in order to get better status for the Son, because the Son is already totally loved by the Father and needs no further security. The Son does not have to go on acting indefinitely; he returns to the Father and 'abides' in the Father. This shows a 'normal' relationship, of purpose and work and security. In this 'normality', it is possible for the Son's work to end in apparent failure, in rejection and death. But because this is done in the security of the Father's sending, it is glorifying.

For Paul and the first Christian teachers, this was the heart of the message, not that this sort of thing had just been splendidly demonstrated by a hero but that this was a way of life which they themselves found themselves able to share. They found that they could take to themselves the kind of language which Jesus used; and they found that this took priority over all the conventional categories and definitions of human membership. They found that the best way of expressing this was to say that God had sent the Spirit of his Son into their hearts.

At the Lambeth Conference, the world-wide get-together of Anglican bishops every ten years, the daily worship is led by different provinces using their local rites, often using regional languages. A good friend who was once a bishop in Central Africa, and was used to worshipping in a variety of languages, commented that there was only one language in which God was addressed as 'Dad', and that was the Welsh. Well, it is true that, in addressing God, the word for Father, 'Tad', is often mutated into 'Dad'; but it is still the routine, formal word for Father; it doesn't signify anything special by way of familiarity. Nor does the normal word for Father in Zulu and Xhosa, 'Baba', which might appear to be very close to the Hebrew 'Abba', the word which Paul quotes and which Jesus used in his praying. But this 'Abba' is a particularly intimate form in Hebrew, the first meaningful sound that a baby makes. It is not the formal word for Father, and some interpreters suggest that the nearest equivalent in English culture would indeed be 'Dad'. But you can't legislate for this, or make a liturgy out of it; it is not devised by human organisation; it is the effect of the Spirit of the Son speaking in our hearts.

It is something which happens when the speaker has reached a certain level of maturity. It is God speaking to God. We see that God is Son, child, as well as Father, parent; that makes a big difference to the way that the image of God registers with us. Disorders in our understandings of God often derive from disordered relationship with our parents. God provides healing, not by demanding changes in our behaviour but by showing that God is more than father. God is on both sides of the parent/child divide. We therefore may find as much insight into the nature of God from our relationships with our children as we do from our relationships with our parents. God is to be known on both sides of the conflict, and in God's own nature God overcomes the conflict. Because God is child, alongside us, speaking in us, we can, without hostility and without guilt and without timidity, pray as the Son has taught us, saying 'Our Father'.

Now Paul is struggling through bracken and squelching through bogland, trying to find ways of reaching to where his Galatians are getting stuck. He fears that his approach to them, and his teaching, may turn out to have been a waste of time.

But he starts again with encouragement, insisting that, in spite of everything, they are still his 'brothers and sisters'. They are still family; they have become like each other. Paul, the teacher, has been doing a lot of becoming. His attempts to be a missionary have deeply changed him. 'I am becoming as you are,' he says (knowing that there will be Jewish Christians who will be accusing him of having simply 'gone native'). 'I have made a move towards you; I beg you to become as I am, to move towards me.' At present, by getting involved with the intricacies of religious laws and exclusive ceremonial, you are moving away from me, you are denying the relationship which has been growing between us. I have been moving into an inclusive fellowship where all that matters is our bond with Jesus Christ; now this is no longer sufficient for you; you are wanting something extra, to be enslaved into a system of exclusive regulations and classifications. As you move in that direction, you are moving to where I used to be.

All this is a great disappointment to Paul. Something has gone wrong. At first, the Galatians had received him very happily, in spite of a disability which might well have made them scorn or despise him; on the contrary, there was evidently something about this disability which made them feel that he was indeed an angel sent from God. So they had received him and welcomed him, and he had become under obligation to them. But now they are treating him as an enemy. What has happened?

Paul's opponents have been operating a subtle kind of evil. They have been playing on the Galatians' anxiety about their identity. Evil searches for a soft spot of insecurity and drills away at it. 'They want you,' Paul says, 'but not in a healthy way. They want to exclude you – on account of your acceptance of the true Gospel of the inclusive and sufficient love of Christ; they want to exclude you so that you may be more attracted to them.' It may seem perverse, but it is alarmingly true to life. The sense of being excluded is a painful one and is calculated to make people feel servile. They are made to feel inadequate and unqualified, and so they are stimulated to seek the qualifications possessed by those who are qualified. This puts them under the domination of those who are qualified and who decide what the qualifications are. So they are kept feeling inferior and indebted. By such means, the disadvantaged are kept disadvantaged, and distances are maintained. This is a kind of slavery from which there will seem to be no escape. Real genuine separation is more healthy than this tantalising, conditional inclusion, which exaggerates the importance of detailed qualifications, sets each of us against our neighbour, and breeds creepers and informers.

Do you see this sort of pattern going on, in churches, offices, colleges, clubs …? It will never be far from home, and it is the devil to get rid of. It certainly put Paul on guard. He was trying to diagnose the trouble from a distance; he had deliberately not stayed hanging around them while they were growing up in faith; but he feels that perhaps he has cut the umbilical cord too early; we may note, incidentally, that he is perfectly able to cut through gender stereotyping and think of himself as a mother.

So Paul takes the line, if you are so keen on being directed by the old law, let's look at what the law actually says. He may even be saying, if you are so keen on the law's culture, let me, as a former expert in it, give you a taste of it, and you can see whether you really want to go down that road. Then, perhaps inspired by his own self-identification as a mother, he gets into this abstruse argument about the two mothers of Abraham's children. Will it 'ring bells' with them? There's no getting away from the sense that characters such as Hagar and Sarai mean very little to western Gentile Christians. However, we need to take seriously the fact that Abraham, the spiritual grandfather of more than half the inhabitants of our planet, can well be reckoned as the most influential person that there has ever been.[43] We Christians may not be passionately concerned about Hagar; but she means a lot to our colleagues in Islam, and in Judaism. In their company, it would be wise for us not to be too loud in our publicising of Paul's particular interpretation of Hagar's role in the story. It will not win us friends, and Paul's main contention can stand without it. It is part of his struggle; and we have no evidence about whether it impressed the Galatians or not.

Paul evidently feels uneasy with his performance in the role of 'mother'; perhaps he would have been happier with being 'father' to his Galatian family, with the authority and ownership which can be expected of the father-figure. But there is something about motherhood which he can't get away from. For this family, he has been that marvellous mechanism which protects, nurtures, and expels the new life. And then his policy in their infancy has been to avoid getting them into an over-dependent relationship, and so he has left them to find maturity in their own resources. But the church there is very young. It depends on the presence of the individual teacher/parent – there are no books of doctrine yet written, not even a collection of notes or letters which could be offered for their sustaining and formation. So, has he been too hasty in leaving them to find their own way? Wouldn't it be good if they could be back in the womb again, so that he could make a better job of it second time round? Not having kids of his own, Paul must have been overhearing some honest conversations between mothers! We readers can simply be grateful that Paul's policy did run into problems; if he had stayed with his young 'family' and seen them through this identity crisis, he would not have had to write, and we would not have *Galatians* in our Bible.

We do not have to follow all the details of Paul's argument about Hagar. The important issue is that there are two kinds of mothering, and these can apply anywhere. There is 'slave-style'; the mother is a slave, engaged for the purpose of producing an offspring, an heir; she is a tool by which the man (in Hagar's case, Abraham) tries to fulfil his own ambitions. She is a component in a project of human engineering. The father is working in non-faith; he experiences the disappointment which comes to those who trust in mechanisms and who seek freedom in the future by practising slavery in the present. Where the mother is enslaved to produce a son, that son is likely to be a slave also. He will be seen as the product of a successful scheme; he will have to fulfil expectations. Organisation man will breed organisation child. The opposite to the 'slave-mother' is the 'free-woman'. Her son is a gift. He is something more than the product of genetic mechanisms or political manipulation. He is the fulfilment of nobody's schemes and ambitions. He is not 'born of the will of the flesh'. He breaks the bounds of expectation, and is accepted as a wonder and a joy. The mothering of such children will allow them to be unpredictable, to be more than what their origin would allow them to be.

Paul's contention is that the Galatians, in their yearning for the discipline of the law of Moses, the law of Sinai, are seeking a conditional relationship with God, a slave-state. In that sort of relationship, the promises are conditional – 'If you do this and that, if you keep the rules, God will keep his part of the bargain and will love you.' But that is not the way of the love of God shown in Christ, experienced by Paul. The love of 'the Son of God who loved me and gave himself for me' is a huge love, which goes beyond duty or reason. It is unconditional, true mother-love. We cannot grow into maturity if our membership and our acceptedness are all in proportion to our 'being good'. We cannot be free if we are constantly checking to see whether our goodness is sufficient to gain the approval of parent, and if we are set in competition for approval by comparison with brother or sister. In the same way, our access (a favourite word in Paul's other writings)[44] to the love of God cannot depend on our 'being correct'. Some arguments about what sort of people can be priests suggest that God is like a reluctant Social Security official, that when we open ourselves to receive what we need he will give it only when all the right boxes have been ticked. That does not fit well with Jesus's own behaviour as the accessible king, the donkey-rider whose eyes are on the same level as the eyes of the pedestrians.[45]

To come at the question from a different angle, Paul now sets up a comparison between two types of city, two explorations of 'Jerusalem'. Like most other citizens of Britain, I have never been to Jerusalem. But neither had most of the Galatians that Paul was writing to. For both of us, 'Jerusalem' is a kind of myth; in that way, we can explore what Paul is referring to in his comparisons.

The contemporary Jerusalem was in bondage in Paul's day; it was occupied by a foreign power, with massive military force and a sophisticated legal and political system; it was the home of the religious inheritance which had nurtured Paul and which so appealed to the distant inhabitants of Galatia; it had been given the opportunity to accept Jesus as Messiah; he had come to it, and there he was crucified. It rejected the opportunity. It could have been the place of fulfilment of the wonderful prophecy of Isaiah, that little Israel could have been the mediator and peacemaker between the two cruel tyrannical nations of enslavement, Egypt and Assyria. It could have become a focus-point for an inclusive human culture.[46] But it could not escape from the claim of the sacrifices made by those who had it made it what it was; it could not face the calling to become something more than what it knew itself to be. It did not know the things that belonged to its peace, and the tears of the

Messiah foretold its destruction.[47] There is still much in Jerusalem today for the Lord to weep for, a location of competitive idolatries, a walled city of control and disappointment, the focus-point for the most intractable and tragic of contemporary political crises. And there is the other 'Jerusalem', the free city. Paul is clear that it does exist. It is a community of peoples of different origins and backgrounds, languages, skills, and cultures, who live by supplying each other's needs. In such a community, distinctions and separations based on ancestry or inherited status are seen as uncivilised. The true city is mother of all its citizens. Membership of this city is a political experience, and the co-operation needed for the city to be true to itself is a political skill. Now, this is not an imaginative city, in Paul's exposition. Nor is it distant, purely spiritual, in the future, beyond death. It is the Jerusalem which is 'above', which has a character of heaven, but is already on earth. Indeed, it is here before us, it is our mother which has given us birth. It is a reality now. It is a community which we can share, which has its own contribution to make to the polis, the political enterprise on earth. It is the disciple-community of the followers of Jesus, the community into which Paul has been attracting the Galatian colleagues.

'Jerusalem', in this sense, is not a very lively part of our currency in this country at this time. But a similar image is very much alive, in our singing of *Cwm Rhondda*, in church and on the field; this is the image of 'Jordan'. 'Jordan', also, is a physical reality and political feature, with a meaning of identity and of separation. But I sing it because it is also about me, my hope and my destination, a boundary which I look forward to crossing at death. But the first singers of songs such as 'Deep River, I want to cross over Jordan' were the black people of the Deep South; for them, 'Jordan' was the Ohio, the boundary between the slave-states and the free. These singers had never been across the Ohio; but they believed in its existence, even though they had not experienced it. 'Deep River', especially as sung by the choirs of the new South Africa, is a song which sums up what Paul is offering as he leads towards his message of Freedom.[48]

Paul has been trying to respond to his readers' sense of insecurity. They feel desolate and barren, unproductive of the achievements of law-abiding behaviour, of success and social credibility, which they can see in the colleagues whose commitment they envy. But God is the master of history, as he was in the days of Abraham; he reverses people's status, and he leads towards freedom. If God be God, God is on your side. Like Isaac, you have been born out of a situation which has looked like one of hopelessness and deadness. But your birth has happened, and is happening, because God is fulfilling his promise. You are the new thing; you are what you are, not because you are simply following the natural process of reproduction, nor because you are climbing on board an ancient tribal system of rules, but because of a new creation. You can try to ignore this, you can refuse it; but it is God's project and God's purpose. You do have the option of entangling yourselves in a mechanism of slavery, but that would be a matter of your deliberate refusal of a pathway of freedom. You cannot be both in and out of such a mechanism. The slave-state of life and the free state of life are irreconcilable. The slave-style will feel threatened by the free and will try to destroy it.

The section of your personality which wants to remain in slavery may well be more energetic than that which is willing to be liberated. But that is not the path that history is destined to follow; the offspring of slavery is doomed. Can you find the good in slavery, or preserve its best values? Liberation is the Creator's purpose and it will be fulfilled. In Christ, freedom is a genuine offer and gift; it cannot be permanently suppressed by its opposite.

QUESTIONS

Slavery – what kinds of slavery do you see in these days, at home, at work, in community-life, in church, internationally?

God as Father, God as Mother, God as Child? How do these ideas of God fit with your understanding and your experience, with your experience of being a child, of being a parent or a guardian or a carer?

Do you have personal experience of adoption? Can you share some of this with other members of your group?

What does this say about our relationship with people who are not of our family?

FOR THANKSGIVING AND PRAYER

Give thanks for Paul, the crosser of boundaries, the awkward one who insisted on his vision even when it put his colleagues in the wrong, the Jew who could sit light to some essential things in his tradition, the Roman citizen, the scholar in Greek, Hebrew and Latin, who could put all that on one side, who could wrestle with tough intellectual questions and expose his inmost feelings and passion, the one who gave us the document we are studying.

Pray for the teachers, the explorers, the translators, the writers of our day, who put us in touch with each other, who enable us to learn from each other's experiences. Pray for the writers and editors of our Christian publications, and for the teachers in our local schools.

STEP 6

Mount Freedom/*Moel Rhyddid*
Galatians 5:1-15

We have been trying to follow Paul through the foggy byways of his symbol-system of motherhood and citizenship. Suddenly, the cloud disperses and he is at a new mountain-top. 'Freedom!' You *are* free. Stand firm in the freedom which you have been given, and don't let yourself get entangled again in any system of enslavement.

Paul is the apostle of freedom. He does not offer a theory of freedom; he is not an establishment figurehead, appealing to the powerful to give a bit more freedom to the powerless. Like Jesus before him, he moves among the powerless themselves, struggling to identify with their motives, frustrations and temptations. He bids the enslaved claim freedom, he bids the disinherited claim an inheritance, which is already theirs. Because of this, Paul became, like Jesus, a victim of counter-revolutionary violence. So he could claim to have been crucified. Paul and his message, we now know, were successful, not through possessing political or military power which could match violence with violence, but because the community of Christ possessed a more effective set of symbols, a more powerful story than the myths and the symbols which inspired the communities of privilege. The community of Christ could live and die in confidence in the dying and rising of Jesus. But Paul has to warn that we abandon this Christ if we allow ourselves to get trapped in a new form of enslavement.

Paul insists that his Galatian friends are free. He does not offer them freedom as the opportunity to choose. He does not invite them to return to a lost freedom. He urges them to *remain in* freedom. Their freedom is not a freedom to choose between freedom and slavery. The freedom to choose is itself a kind of bondage; you cannot move while you are undecided, with a choice between two roads at a junction, or with a choice between two people to marry. The only freedom that you have then is a freedom to dither and delay, to engage in hourly re-appraisal or in routine situation-analysis, to do anything but actually do something. Freedom to choose can be a delusion, a choice between being eaten by a lion called Leo or by a lion called Cleo. It can be a device to catch you into someone's schemes, an excuse for proliferating almost identical alternative products to feed a market of waste. This may be attractive for the privileged and sophisticated, but it is no use in face of the real traps and crises. You are free once the choice is made; you are able to travel down the chosen road, to commit to the chosen person.

But the freedom that Paul is speaking of is neither the freedom of being able to choose, nor even the freedom of having chosen; it is the freedom of *having been chosen*. It is the freedom of grace, of having been adopted and given freedom as children of God. It is the freedom which you have when your life-partner says 'I will'. From outside, it may look like another form of enslavement. But to live in order to acquire valuedness is enslavement: to live with a given valuedness is freedom, because one's security is already established.

You are free. You have been set free. Christ has made you free. The enslaving power has no hold on you any longer. You are no longer its victim. So let go of the consciousness of being a victim. Some individuals, and some national groups, find it difficult to relinquish their status as victims; being a victim gives excuse for competitiveness, for paranoia, for idleness. But that means that you are giving your enslaver a continuing power over yourself; and you are failing to recognise, and give thanks for, the grace of your liberator. You are returning to slavery. Certainly, remember that you were a slave; but, in the Hebrew Scriptures, the reason for doing so is so that you may care for those who now are slaves, strangers, aliens.[49]

There is no purpose in being freed. For *freedom* Christ has freed you – not for any scheme or mechanism, not so that you can set up a whole new set of goals and targets to achieve in competition with others. Those who are enslaved exist to satisfy purposes. If there is to be freedom for them, it must come as a gift, not as part of a new system. It will be redemption. And it can be found within a situation of enslavement, of loss of freedom. Paul himself knew this. When he was behind bars, he could sing, pray, sleep, while those who kept him behind bars had to be totally committed to keeping him behind bars.

During the apartheid regime, we had friends who were under banning orders, deprived of most of the normal forms of freedom, freedom of association, freedom of mobility. What is to be said to such a person? Do we say, 'We are sorry that you are not free now, but you should look forward to being free in five years' time'? Surely, at the risk of sounding complacent or callous, we have to say, 'You are free, you are where you are because you are free. Hold on to that freedom, and don't let them get away with enslaving you.' We are made for freedom, and that is why the tyrants are doomed. Paul's statement about freedom is addressed to people who were still, in hard and unyielding practice, slaves. For them, as much as for anyone, it was true; you have a freedom which no one can take away from you.

There is that core of freedom in the human spirit in defiance of circumstance and fate, such as was identified by Viktor Frankel among some of his companions in Auschwitz, when he observed that 'forces beyond your control can take away everything that you possess except one thing, the last of the human freedoms – to choose one's attitude in any given set of circumstances, to choose one's own way'.[50] It was, in a very different setting, the freedom such as my wife was able to explore with inmates when she served as an educational visitor in a British prison. Such a freedom establishes the difference between survival and death. And this is worked out and put into a new and eternal narrative in the claims of Jesus as redeemer.

But the free people will probably find that they are a minority. Once they start to express their freedom in caring ways, they will run into boundaries. We can test the claims of a community to be freedom-loving by noticing the kind of people that it restricts, and the kind of obstructions that they encounter when they try to love their neighbours in any practical ways. As the Church of England bishops' Pastoral Letter pointed out, when the press and public figures go on about recipients of benefit as undeserving 'scroungers', ordinary citizens feel discouraged from getting concerned even about the most vulnerable. The maintainers of enslavement are not in uniform. A police state is not a state in which there are crowds of obvious policemen at every street corner; it is a state in which many members of the public have allowed themselves to become unpaid and un-uniformed policemen.

Paul does not go off into sublime theories about freedom. He is where he is because of a specific issue involving specific people. They are being attracted into a programme of getting extra insignia and identity in addition to their identity in baptism and in Christ. They are in danger of becoming enslaved into the culture of circumcision, and that is an issue which is not going away. It's not that circumcision is a bad thing in itself; for those who are by background and tradition children of the Jewish law it is not a problem. But to seek it as a new requirement, as a more advanced kind of membership beyond our commitment to Christ, that is to make Christ redundant, and to submit oneself to the whole apparatus of the Jewish law. Those who deliberately become circumcised will find that they are trapped in commitment to a tyrant with insatiable demands.

Once you give authority to this way of measuring people in terms of their conformity to a set of rules and qualifications you find that your whole ability to make judgements gets corrupted. The moment of becoming committed to this way of being yourself is critical. To attempt to get yourself into extra favour with God by improving your qualifications is to reject Christ's work of salvation. You are looking for something which you can claim for yourself, a qualification or achievement which you can feel belongs to you. But what Christ gives is not something that you can grasp and call your property; the righteousness, the sense of being truly related to God, is not a property, it is a hope. Hope is what we wait for. Power or truth or wealth are things which we can possess; they have limits and boundaries. But love is not love unless there is more love to come. We will never feel that it is complete. That is why hope and love are eternally linked together. And they are linked in freedom, which also exists in hope.

Black students in South Africa had never known any form of education other than the ideologically constructed and deliberately limiting system known as Bantu Education; but they knew that they were being cheated, that something better could be available, better than anything that they had experienced, an education in freedom and for freedom. It could not be proved or demonstrated; but it was true.[51] At a time when the situation in Northern Ireland was especially bleak and discouraging, we in the Wilfred Owen Association invited the Irish poet Seamus Heaney to come to Shrewsbury to address us. I do not remember his address, but I do remember his response to a question about whether he was optimistic about the future of Northern Ireland: 'Optimism says, we are going to win. Hope says, what we are doing is worth doing. I have hope.' This agrees with the contention of Vaclav Havel, the dramatist and philosopher, who became president of Czechoslovakia after the collapse of Soviet domination: 'Hope is not the conviction that something will turn out well, but the certainty that something makes sense regardless of how it turns out.'

Paul could not have known whether his mission with the Galatians would turn out well; but he knew that, in the resurrection of Jesus, nothing is wasted.[52] That is the basis of our belief in freedom. We stand in freedom for God's justice, both waiting for it and working to hasten it,[53] being content with limited horizons and being ready for an invisible future.

Perhaps you will let me add two other examples from South Africa. In 1969, when the cruelties of the apartheid system were getting steadily worse, one weekend we ran a racially-inclusive conference in Johannesburg; it was supposed to be about the 'generation gap', but inevitably focussed upon the worsening political situation. I was offering an exercise in exploring people's hopes, and it was all pretty gloomy. At one point, I was with a little group of African journalists. And the question was, in effect, 'what on earth is this country going to be like in twenty-five years time, if things go on as they are doing now?' One of them said straight, 'In twenty-five years time, South Africa will be a free non-racial democracy.' The others said, 'That's crazy; what possible evidence do you have?' His answer was, 'It simply can't go on like it is; it will have to change; in twenty-five years time, it will have changed.' From then on, I counted the years; 25 years brought us to 1994 – Mandela President!

In 1960, the Rev. C.F. Beyers Naudé was head of the Nederduitse Gereformeerde Kerk – virtually archbishop – of the Transvaal, the church which traditionally supported the government's apartheid policy. He came out in opposition to that policy, and was dismissed from his ministry. He became leader of the Christian Institute, struggling for the true Gospel in the face of the forces of heresy and injustice. Journalists from Europe and the USA came visiting us in our churches; their question was, 'How do you keep going? What is the point of your struggle, when everywhere everything is going against you?' The journalists would get out their notebooks and tape recorders, to catch Beyers's reply. It was very simple, 'Christ is risen.'

To return to the detail of Paul's argument. Circumcision, in itself, is not an evil thing; it is an indifferent thing. And the same is true of uncircumcision. Those who, through no choice of their own, have been circumcised, are no worse for that. But no one should take pride in their uncircumcision. That is not an alternative badge of value. 'Uncircumcision' can be a source of pride, a boasting of freedom from rules and religions and rituals. There can be competition between those who want to be 'more uncircumcised than thou', scoring points on a ladder of who is most secular and unbound by convention. In the search for this kind of new sectional security, they can breed as much anxiety and bondage to slogans as any 'conservative' body. Anarchism and counter-dependence can be as enslaving as conformism and subservience to authority. Ideological circumcision and ideological uncircumcision both keep people in a state where they are vulnerable prey for demagogues and rogues. They march in step with each other, like a prisoner falling in step with his guard.

What is motivating these people towards rejecting their freedom? What is the attraction of yielding oneself to an authoritarian system? It is one solution to the common feeling of being alone and insignificant. Freedom comes as loss of support and security, and is then a threat rather than a blessing – a burden and a grief at a time of social or cultural or personal upheaval. People are attracted by the prospect of withdrawing into immaturity and submitting to a safe system. It seems that Paul's readers in Galatia have been caught into a state of this kind, to judge from his understanding of their trouble and his attempts to respond. No-tice that, although he speaks of the power of God's call to himself, he avoids any stress on the almightiness or dominion of Jesus. He does not try to get his readers to surrender their personalities to a master-Christ. Indeed, he makes very little reference to Jesus's theme of 'the Kingdom of God'. He stresses the aspects of faith which are based on personal value – the Son of God who loved me and gave himself for me. His readers are in danger of surrendering their lives and identities to an ex-ternalised system; this would be even worse if it were to be replaced by a demand to surrender to Christ. The cure is not to find a better power to which to surrender. Christ is the answer, not because he is the ideal tyrant but because he is the model of liberty.

Christ's apostle has to represent this model himself, in his efforts to persuade and to free the minds of those whom he calls his brothers and sisters. So he stresses his confidence in them. In a situation of strain and fear, where people are setting up standards and are suspicious of each other's loyalty, it becomes difficult to trust others, because I know that I am myself not trusted. The remedy can come if someone can reliably and credibly convince me that they have faith in me. So while Paul argues with them about their problem, he makes it clear that he distin-guishes them from the person or persons who are causing the problem. He avoids making the sort of comment which would only intensify their guilt. 'It takes only a small amount of yeast to leaven the whole batch of dough' – the source of the trouble may be very small. But the person who is causing the trouble – perhaps just a single person – will carry the responsibility. It is the stimulator of the disorder, rather than the mis-guided victims, who will have to face the burden of scrutiny and evalu-ation. 'I am confident that you can distinguish between the voice of the one who has called you and the voice that is causing you such trouble. For the one who is causing you this trouble, it would be best for him to go all the way and castrate himself – that would be the end of his fruit-fulness!'

Christ is freedom. Christ is the free person, and he showed his free-dom by his refusal to be diverted from his path of commitment to the purpose of God, even to the point of being rejected by the law of state, the law of religion, and by public opinion, and being crucified. That freedom was affirmed by the Creator in the sign that death could not enslave him. That is Christ's freedom. You were called to freedom, to exercise your freedom as the Spirit of Jesus enables you to be free as Jesus was free, in love and service of each other.

There follows the obvious question: Freedom for what? 'Freedom', like 'justice', is a notion that is vulnerable to being taken over by our own self-interest. 'Freedom of speech', the 'free market', 'free choice' can easily be taken as licence for the powerful to strengthen their power in their own interest; and that is just another form of slavery. In their enthusiasm to be consumers, they end up as consumers of each other.

This is not just a modern problem. Nearly 500 years ago, Martin Luther saw freedom as, in the first instance, deliverance from the rules and regulations and qualification-system of the Church of Rome. But he had to wrestle with the misuse of this vision of freedom. It's worth quoting him in full, with the asides and diversions that he gets up to:

> *Christians do gladly receive and obey this doctrine* [that liberty is fulfilled in the mutual love within the community]. *Others, as soon as liberty is preached, by and by do thus infer: If I be free, then I may do what I list; this thing is mine own, why then should I not sell it for as much as I can get? Moreover, seeing we obtain not salvation by our good works, why should we give anything to the poor? Thus do they most carelessly shake off the yoke of the law of love, and turn the liberty of the Spirit into wantonness and fleshly liberty. But we will tell such careless contemners (although they believe us not, but laugh us to scorn), that if they use their bodies and their goods after their own lust (as indeed they do, for they neither help the poor, nor lend to the needy, but beguile their brethren in bargaining, snatching and scraping unto themselves by hook or by crook whatsoever they can get) we tell them (I say) that they be not free, brag they never so much of their liberty, but have lost Christ and Christian liberty, are become bondslaves of the devil, and are seven times worse under the name of Christian liberty than they were before under the tyranny of the Pope.*[54]

Somehow, it doesn't seem a thousand miles away from London – or from Cardiff, for that matter! Indeed, it recalls, from a further thousand years earlier, St Augustine's shrewd recollection of his childhood: 'We enjoyed playing games, and were punished for them by men who were playing games themselves. However, grown-up games are known as "business", and even though boys' games are much the same, they are punished for them by their elders. No one pities either the boys or the men, though surely we deserved pity, for I cannot believe that a good judge would approve of the beatings that I received as a boy on the ground that my games delayed my progress in studying subjects which would enable me to play a less creditable game later in life. Was the master who beat me very different from me?'[55] Oh dear! Poor little Augustine, having to come to terms with the violence of unrestrained capitalism at the age of seven!

The test of our freedom is whether it works out in loving our neighbour. If it enables us to exploit the neighbour who is already at a disadvantage, and to increase that disadvantage, that is not the freedom of Christ; it is extending the regime of slavery. If we use our freedom of speech in defence of those who do not have effective voice, that is in accordance with Christ's freedom; but if we use it to boost our own self-satisfaction by exposing someone else to ridicule, that devalues the whole notion of freedom and therefore extends the regime of slavery, however clever our arguments or our cartoons may be. In short, freedom is falsely claimed unless it is being used in solidarity with those who are un-free, unless it is being used in harmony with God's purpose of liberation. It is freedom to love, not a base-camp from which to pursue what Paul calls the works of 'the flesh'. To live according to 'the flesh' is slavery; it is to let things happen according to the impersonal mechanisms of the market; it is unredeemed living, moral abdication. It is to rest in a definition of myself which alleges that I am only what the impersonal economic or social mechanisms have made me.

At one stage in the struggle in South Africa, there were persuasive voices telling us not to waste our energy in protest or in caring for the oppressed, because apartheid was economic nonsense and would eventually disappear. True, it was economic nonsense; but it would have been quite wrong, quite un-free, for us to sit quietly on one side, impervious to the anger and oppression, waiting for impersonal forces to do what conscience and political action should have been doing.

There is indeed a law, a commandment; but it is not a long list of rules by which you can assess your performance and that of your colleague. It is simple and single, loving your neighbour as yourself. In such loving, we each affirm our own value and that of the other person. Where this is not happening, we pursue a value for ourselves, in separation from the other; our search for status is in compensation for our own unlovedness. That is the danger for the Galatians. You are loved, Paul insists, this lovedness is the truest thing about you, as it is the truest thing about me – the Son of God who loved me and gave himself for me. To refuse to love what God loves is to reject God's own generosity. In this sense, the commandment of law is freedom, a powerful blessing to the world.

The opposite of this is when we become a prey for each other. Other people are used as stepping-stones in pathways of ambition. The uncircumcised are a prey for the circumcised, and vice versa. The whole Galatian crisis could be described as spiritual cannibalism. It is incompatible not only with loving one's neighbour but with loving oneself. To fatten oneself on the flesh of others is self-destructive, rooted in self-hatred. It is based on the assumption that one has value only in comparison with someone else's lack of value. In such circumstances, neither of us can win; as Gandhi and Martin Luther King affirmed, we must live together as brothers or die together as fools.[56]

Like all competitiveness, the competitiveness of religion demands resources. It is for the non-poor. This was seen so clearly by that creative reconciler, 20th-century 'man of Galilee', Fr Elias Chacour, Palestinian Arab, citizen of Israel, poor parish priest and school-builder who was called to be Archbishop of Galilee. He noted the various systems and devices by which Christians have tried to decorate their faith; if Christ is not enough, the extras which we load onto him serve only to obscure the truth. 'Christians have wanted to be distinguished and famous instead of using the light in such a way that people can see past us and discover their saviour. I can hear the Third World, the non-Christian world, saying, "Yes, you Christians may be the light, but please dim your headlights, you are blinding us with your brightness, we can no longer see the way, we cannot see where we are going because of your blinding light. Allow us to see your Lord. Dim your lights."'[57]

The lure of circumcision can take many forms. Like circumcision itself, they may, for some people, be legitimate, things to take pride in, or, in Paul's word, to 'boast' of. But.... Our concern for good order, in structure and in worship, can conceal a preference for law over gospel. Our cultural standards can come across as the effortless superiority of an aristocracy. Our sense of humour can be a curtain for excluding those who don't share our in-group references. All these, and many more, *can* be developing truly from our creative freedom. Or they *can* be devices of our fear of freedom, infecting other people with such fear, and obscuring the figure of Christ. If in doubt, dim.

QUESTIONS

This question right through *Galatians:* Is Christ enough? One answer has been, No; we want something more definite, something more exclusive, we want circumcision, with all the rules and regulations attached.

Is Christ enough for you? Or is Christ the old thing, redundant, no longer fulfilling?

In Christianity as you experience it nowadays, what might correspond to 'circumcision'? What functions as exclusiveness, as providing an extra in-group qualification for special people?[58]

FOR THANKSGIVING AND PRAYER

The churches of the Reformed traditions, and especially the Lutherans, will, in 2017, be celebrating the 500th anniversary of Martin Luther's 'theses', which had the effect of setting the Reformation in motion.

So, give thanks for Martin Luther, and his colleagues, who almost 'rediscovered' the importance of Paul's writings; for Luther's commitment to freedom of conscience, and his concern for the 'poor afflicted conscience'; for his willingness to take a stand against oppression and exploitation. Give thanks for faithful Christians in Germany of the 20th century, such as Dietrich Bonhoeffer, executed by the Nazis a few weeks before VE Day, and his colleague Martin Niemöller, who was a great inspiration to us in South Africa; at a time when the official German church failed to distinguish between Christian tradition and national ambition, they remained faithful to the Gospel.

Pray for clearness of vision, for ourselves and our churches, in making that same distinction; and for our politicians in UK and Europe, that they may maintain the structures that have been built to preserve peace in Europe, and be creative in response to new circumstances and opportunities.

STEP 7

Back on level ground
Galatians 5:16 – 6:10

A problem about a word. Fourteen times in *Galatians* Paul uses the Greek word *sarx,* which is normally translated 'flesh'. There is a real difficulty here, and many modern translations try different solutions. We are coming to Paul's list of 'the works of the flesh'; it is clear that he includes activities which are entirely non-material, like jealousy. So he not referring only to activities of a physical type. To translate 'flesh' by 'human nature' implies that the nature of humanity is naturally opposed to the purpose of the Creator; in that case, it could not have been claimed for the life of the Son of God. 'Lower nature' implies that a person can be divided into sections, that I *have* them rather than that I *am* them. The NRSV decides, I think rightly, that it is best to share the problem with the reader, to let the awkward word 'flesh' stand and let the reader discover the meaning from the actual use that Paul is making of the word. By 'flesh', he is meaning the whole bundle of powers that are hostile to freedom, to love, and to the Spirit. Some of its activities are indeed physical, some spiritual, some individual, some social. 'Flesh' is a moral term, not a psychological term. It is not about a section of me or a possession or an aspect of me; it is about the whole of me – body, mind, imagination, will, – operating contrary to love and to Spirit.

Paul is gradually coming down from the mountain to a level place, where issues of behaviour and conduct have to be worked out in practice. But these moral questions are dealt with only after the grounds for personal security have been spelled out, only when it is clear that obedience is going to be a matter of freedom and not of arbitrary compulsion. Otherwise, the comparisons of good and bad behaviour would merely stimulate all the old motives of comparison and self-justification.

Paul does not say, 'Be good and don't be bad.' There is just one imperative, 'Walk by the Spirit, and then you will not be driven by the demands of flesh.' When your life is a battleground between flesh and Spirit, you are frustrated, you cannot do the good things which you wish to do. Equally, you fail to do the bad things that you wish to do. Such people have so much conflict in their situation that their energies are spent not in activity but in resistance to activity; they are not free to be either good nor bad. All possible courses of action have something

wrong about them. And this could be where the Galatians find themselves. Their awareness of the law leaves them depressed, with conscience as a burden. Conscience can block action, by demanding that a
'good' or 'bad' label has to be given to every possibility. This can be the
biggest obstacle to creative freedom; it therefore serves as a convenient
device for those who want to avoid change.

Those who are led by Spirit are saved not only from flesh but also
from law. Law does not save from flesh; it is flesh's ally. Law and flesh
both seek to give us satisfaction and assurance in terms of our security in
comparison with other people's insecurity. Law would seek to oppose
flesh by building up a good stock of long-service–and–good-conduct
medals. But this serves only to give new life to the old trouble. The real
opposite to evil is not virtue but Spirit; and Spirit does not have 'works'
or 'activities' which can be quantified. It bears fruit, which is a different
kind of thing altogether from the activities of flesh.

Spirit is opposite to flesh. It is the authentic way of being human.
Spirit is the Spirit of God's Son, sharing with us the voice and the motives of the Son. In so far as we are led by Spirit, or walk by Spirit (Paul
switches very easily from 'the Spirit' to 'Spirit') we will not fulfil the
desires of flesh and also not be subject to law. We will be free. Thus Paul
completes his pattern of terminology: Spirit, faith, and freedom are different aspects of a divine strategy which is opposed to a hostile strategy
characterised by flesh, law, and slavery.

To walk by Spirit does not mean that flesh and its motivations are
abolished. To the depressed or troubled conscience (for which Martin
Luther had constant sympathy) this statement is not a further burden but
a lifting of the gloom. The conflict which we experience is not a sign of
our inexcusable badness; it is the common lot of the Christian disciple,
and, in one sense, it is nothing to worry about. The person who is really
aware of the way of the Spirit will perceive all the more sharply the
motivations and lures of flesh. The Christian does not rest in permanent
innocence, but creatively pushes back the boundaries of chaos, turns de-
pression and failure into hope, and knows the secret whereby sin can be
a way in to new righteousness. Paul can look this conflict in the face,
not because he can rely on his own innocence but because he knows
himself to be forgiven and accepted. Where God is known to be forgiving, law loses its threat. Where God is known to be forgiving, the
maintenance of human classifications on a moral basis becomes absurd.
The past loses its power to decide who we are and where we must be.
Where God is known to be forgiving, we can be free to walk by the
Spirit.

The meaning of 'flesh' becomes clearer when we see Paul's list of specimens. Some of these are activities of sensual lust, such as prostitution (the literal meaning of the first on the list), and licentiousness. The impersonal exploitation of another person's body is against the motive of Spirit, because it separates the action of the body from the inter-personal commitment which it should signify – the other person isn't around afterwards. The 'flesh' dehumanises something which is human and corrupts something which is good; it causes us to divert from our humanity, using sexuality as a form of flight from Spirit rather than as a form of involvement with Spirit.

Then there are activities of 'flesh' which are forms of political lust, egocentric aggressiveness and competitiveness, the kind of ambition which cannot tolerate anyone having more than me. These are social as well as individual disorders, power-games, manipulation of people's loyalties, the spreading of factionalism and dissension, whether in family, church, or nation. This also is flight from Spirit, pressing us into excessive concern for success, and anxiety about who is above me and who is below me. But, as with sex, the thing-in-itself is good. Power is a blessing. We are given it, entrusted with it, as a blessing for the whole of the creation. But when it is used divisively and in exploitation, it is part of the working of 'flesh'.

And then there some activities of 'flesh' which are about religious or intellectual lust, such as idolatry and witchcraft. Idolatry is essentially sectional and exclusive; its whole point is that the idol takes my side, and I do my best to ensure that it is stronger than the idol on your side, It will serve my interests, whether it is a 'primitive' fish-god or a sophisticated structure of speculative theory which is accessible only to people who have gone a long way through the filter-system of educational privilege. Witchcraft is a secret system whereby knowledge is reserved for a small in-group and used by them to control the fate of others. So we acquire specialist knowledge and release it to the public only when this will serve our private gain. So these activities may operate in the non-material world, and even refer to 'God'; but they are 'flesh', because they oppose the purposes of Spirit. The 'god' of idolatry and witchcraft is very far removed from the God who is known as Father of our Lord Jesus Christ. Devotion to such a god encourages us to believe that life is basically a matter of manipulation or clever tricks, of being one-up on our intellectual or spiritual rivals.

All this is opposite to 'Spirit', for Spirit is the Spirit of Jesus. Jesus did not pursue or find an escape-route in terms of his success or his performance in competition with others. The Son of God, who loved me and gave himself for me, leads us in an altogether different direction. The

lust for sensory satisfaction, the lust for power, the lust for religious dominance, were the options which Jesus rejected at the beginning of his
ministry; they were evasions of his calling and were opposed to his Spirit.
From then on, his face was set towards Jerusalem, the place of conflict,
dread and death. The seductions of 'flesh' had no power to divert him
from his life in the Spirit.[59]

Paul ends his list by an 'etcetera'; these activities are just representative. But those who go in for such behaviour exclude themselves from
the Kingdom of God. They keep themselves in slavery; as slaves, they
do not inherit. This is not a punishment for making the wrong choice;
it is part of the choice itself.

Of 'flesh' there are 'works' – activities, behaviours. Can we make a
similar list concerning 'Spirit'? That is not Paul's way. Unlike conventional moralists, he does not offer a check-list of sins with their corre-
sponding virtues. The remedy against 'flesh' is not a rival kind of
performance. 'Spirit' is not about doing things. 'Spirit' simply produces
'fruit'. Fruit comes by the slow and hidden process of germination, infancy, growth, adolescence, maturity. There may be flowers on the way;
but the signs of Spirit are fruitful living in line with the Spirit of Jesus.

Jesus himself was, of course, very fond of botanical imagery. To judge
from his parables, his favourite subjects at school would have been
botany and economics. Mary Magdalene's identification of him as the
gardener had a curious appropriateness. But the imagery of growth and
fruitful maturity has its limitations; it obviously has something to do with
age; but that is not to say that the Spirit works only in the over-forties.
Paul's list of works of 'flesh' includes old people's sins. His movement,
in its day, was essentially a young movement, attacking the calculating
morality, the dependence on ancestry, the traditionalist calculations derived from old laws and backward-looking vision. Paul was offering wisdom and maturity in the voice of a cocky young upstart.

'Forbearance', or 'patience', is a gift of maturity, It means rejecting
the weapons which my enemy puts into my hand, refusing to be infected
by the enemy's hostility. It is the central secret of non-violence. It means
overcoming my own impulses of revenge. But the old are not necessarily
more forbearing than the young; those who are least forbearing will be
those who have got most used to implementing the lusts of power.

Humility is another example of fruit. It happens when I stop valuing
myself in terms of the privileges which I have in comparison with others.
My value depends on what I share with others, not on what I have
achieved in competition with others. Only through this sort of humility
can the more privileged persons be free to identify with the oppressed
and the poor, to share their situation and their pain and struggle. Other–
wise, their intervention is another kind of boasting or imperialism. And

oppressed people themselves have humility if they fight in the knowledge that they are fundamentally valued already, not in order to acquire value; they can fight without losing integrity.

Paul's final example of 'fruit' is 'self-control'. This is the opposite of slavery, where one is dominated by someone else's possessiveness and will. It means being able to make one's own judgements, neither in infantile enslavement to authority nor in adolescent rejection of authority. I take responsibility for my own conscience, I do not hand it over to a political or religious or cultural management. I can hear and care for the other person without being dominated by my own anxieties. I do not hand my energies over to prejudices or to drugs – I keep myself free to be able to love my neighbour reliably. So, the fruit of the Spirit is a gift of self-government, a model of valid independence.

Against gifts of this kind, law is powerless and irrelevant. They cannot be organised or prevented by systems or managements. The works of the flesh can, where necessary, be translated into terms which can be assessed in legal fashion, but the fruit of the Spirit cannot be. The most that law can do is to permit the good to be. Law can have a slight role in favour of Spirit; against Spirit it can have no valid role at all.

Paul has finished his mountaineering. He is back home at sea-level, getting on with domestic chores. But this is no after-thought. This is where Practice interpretation gets into gear.

In the light of all that has been discovered at the mountain-top, how do we cope with the gremlins, the snags, the plain awkward things that go wrong through human failings? Competitiveness and envy thrive on the disclosure of other people's weaknesses. When we are steered by 'flesh', we are delighted to discover what is wrong in other people. It helps us to cope with our own sense of inferiority. Bad news becomes good news. The possibility of some intervention which would reduce this badness is unwelcome. The worst news would be that there will be no more bad news. Where there is no bad news, the media perish.

Here is the test of whether we are led by Spirit. Gentleness is a gift of the Spirit. If someone is caught in the act of some kind of lapse from right conduct, you who are of the Spirit should act in a Spirit of gentleness. You should repair that person, like you would treat a broken bone. And watch out – there is probably nothing very exceptional about the culprit, and you are not fireproof yourself. The helper and the helped belong together in the community.

At this deceptively simple point, we meet one of the sharpest forms of disorder in the Christian community, a point at which the whole message of *Galatians* provides a focus of judgement. One of the most

universal characteristics of the church, bridging all divisions of denomi-
nation and tradition, is that we keep each other in business by exposing
each other's vulnerability, 'rejoicing in iniquity'. Censoriousness could
be the single worst disease of the church, more dangerous than formal
disunity, more unconscious than more obvious moral failings. It is to be
found among 'liberals' and 'conservatives' in equal measure. Those who
claim to be permissive are often no more tolerant than their opponents
– they merely choose different targets. And all this is because our interest
in being good is greater than our interest in God.

Those who live by the Spirit will be mindful of what unites them,
and this will be more important than what separates them. This is not
just a matter of the differences of background, race, wealth, or education.
The most serious difference is the moral difference. The moral offender,
particularly the one who is publicly caught out, betrays the fellowship;
the pressure to distance ourselves from this offender is very powerful. If
we are steered by 'the flesh', the best response that we can make is,
'There but for the grace of God am I.' But this is a low valuing of the
grace of God, if all that the grace of God can do is to save us from being
conspicuously bad. Paul is asking his readers to look at the offender and
say, 'There, *because of* the grace of God, *am* I.' That is my brother, my
sister. Their burden is mine. This may look like condoning evil and
abandoning the standards by which life should be regulated. But it is part
of fulfilling the law of Christ, the law of the Son of God who loved me
and gave himself for me. For we have to love people as they actually are,
not as we would have designed them. We have to love the real church,
as it is, and not an ideal dream of what should be. If we want to put
things right in church or society, we need to check that we are not more
in love with our dream than we are with the real people that we claim
to care for. This calls for self-control, another gift of the Spirit, a disci-
plining of visioning and imagination.

Make a realistic evaluation of your role and your work, Paul says, and
do not rely on public opinion. Other people may compare you with
your colleagues, either to your credit or your discredit. But it does not
matter much whether you are a better manager than Mrs A or a worse
public speaker than your predecessor. If you evaluate yourself in that sort
of way, you are mentally enslaving Mrs A or your predecessor to take
responsibility for your standards of assessment. You are making them
carry a burden of responsibility which is properly yours. The only comparison which is valid is the comparison between the you that is and the
you that could be, between the actual you and the potential you. This
is not a matter of self-accusation; it is encouragement, keeping in touch
with God's design for you.

Paul is all the time addressing the community, the brother-sisters, who are a working team. We are given to each other by an authority which is higher than our own choosing. So we bear one another's burdens, because we belong together. Apart from sport, for many of us our best training in team work has come through service in the Armed Forces. One of the most moving and effective depiction of team-work, burden-sharing, is in the Armed Forces Memorial at Alrewas. There are many War Memorials across the country which, for me, say very little. This one is far and away the most meaningful memorial that I know, designed by Ian Rank-Broadley, fabricated at the foundry in Llanrhaeadr ym Mochnant. It speaks beyond words, of the pain, the effort, the value, the community of burden-sharing.

We carry the burdens of each other; each person must carry their own load. Not a contradiction. The words correctly translate a difference in the Greek. The 'burden' is, as in the Armed Forces Memorial, the sheer heavy weight of a colleague's woundedness or deadness; it is the weight of the one which we have to carry as a team. The 'load' is different. It is the cargo that a ship is designed to carry, without which it will bob about uncontrollably on the water. It is the soldier's back-pack. It is the duty which every responsible person should accept. To love means to carry another's burden; it also means to let the other person carry their own proper load. The distinction is very practical.

As helpers, we need to check our own anxieties. Our anxieties about our time, our energy, about public opinion, about health and safety regulations, and half a hundred other things, may discourage us from being available to be burden-sharers. Equally, our anxiety to prove our commitment, to keep ourselves in business, to avoid silence, can make us self-important interferers, trying to stop people taking responsibility for carrying their proper loads. Paternalistically or proprietorially or pauperisingly or patronisingly, we find ourselves insulting young people, old people, disabled people, black people, excusing them from responsibility. Discernment means not being steered by our own anxieties, and being confident in the value which we don't have to earn, the value placed on us by the Son of God who loved me and gave himself for me.

A specific practical example of responsibility for the domestic chores. In the community, there are those who teach and those who are being taught. The responsibility of the teacher is obvious. There is also a responsibility on the person being taught; the literal meaning of the phrase is 'the catechumen' – the person being prepared for baptism. The catechumen is entering a community of mutual responsibility, and is encouraged to see the teacher as a sister or brother with burdens to be shared. We start to take responsibility even when we are under instruction, in a community of shared wealth. Teacher and learner are not polarised against each other; they belong together, and at any time they may find that they are exchanging roles. In referring to the one who teaches, Paul is concerned about the person who fulfils a task, not a person who happens to have a special, superior status. He is not thinking of the well-being of ministers of religion as such, but to ensure that education does not go by default. The church needs to ensure that there is time and space, skills and resources, for the sharing of information, experience and wisdom, for members of the body to learn from each other, so that there is no separation of the 'scholar' from the 'peasant'.

In the business of the church, Paul is concerned that we should not be too much worried about results. He is not interested in immediate league-tables. 'Think not of the harvest but only of proper sowing.' 'Flesh' and 'Spirit' both show results over a period of time, and these results cannot be hastened artificially. The cosmos is not ultimately absurd. We are not victims of some supernatural confidence-trick. This is our hope; as we have already noted, Paul puts our little struggles into a universal perspective; after his piling up of glorious phrases about the triumph of God and the supreme meaning of resurrection, he concludes: 'Get on with what you are doing, because what you do in the Lord is never wasted.'[43]

So, after all, our task is to do good. Very simple. And I wonder whether time spent on books like this might not have been better spent on some more immediate ways of 'doing good'.

But then there is an extra note. We are to do good especially for those of the family of faith. Is this the old exclusiveness coming in at the back door? But this whole section has been about the domestic life of the community; and that has its proper place. The Christian mission is not just a way of universal benevolence; it is a new community based on a family relationship with God through Jesus. To live by faith is to live by the vision of God's purpose for the entire world. A group of people with such a vision certainly needs to have a wide concern for the world outside itself; but precisely for this reason it has a responsibility for itself as well. As well as a welcoming openness, we need to have a cherishing closeness. The management of the garage has to look after the garage roof as well as servicing the vehicles that come in for repair. The Christian community has a task-responsibility, but it also has a maintenance-responsibility. If it is careless about its domestic life, it is not going to be much use to the rest of the world. Those of its members who are engaged in service to the world around, in caring, in conflict, in struggle, need support, need opportunity for sharing their stories, their puzzles, disappointments and joys. There is space, and time for silence, in the family of faith.

QUESTIONS

'We live in a free country.' Do we? What kind of freedom do we look for, if we look for a free society?

What are the implications of *Galatians* for our choices as citizens? How could these be translated into issues for a general election?

What are the implications of *Galatians* for our life together as a church?

What messages would we want to convey to
> Our local parish priest or minister?
> Our local church council?
> Our community council, parish council, town council, MP?

What new commitment should we undertake in our own pilgrimage?

FOR THANKSGIVING AND PRAYER

Take some time to recall significant things that you have learned during this study-programme, and be thankful.

Go over your answers to the last group of questions; dedicate yourselves to some specific actions, praying for yourselves and your colleagues in your local community.

SEND-OFF

Galatians 6:11–18
Final Summary

This is for you.

So, that's the end of the message.

But Paul has started with a personal statement, and he finishes in a similar way. He wants to make sure that his readers will realise that it is Paul himself speaking, not a spin-doctor or Personal Assistant or secretary, but the Apostle himself. A secretary would write neatly, with due care not to waste paper. Paul spreads himself; he writes big.

He summarises his message: don't be tricked by all the arguments in favour of circumcision. The people who are trying to get you into their schemes do so only because they want you as scalps, so that they can put up a good show. They want to feel successful, in their attempts to inveigle you into their schemes They are afraid that if they do not put up a good performance as effective agents of the circumcision business, they will be identified as servants of the cross of Christ and be persecuted for that reason. These people who are being circumcised do not cherish the law (note again that Paul is not attacking those who have been circumcised in the past, who would include faithful Christian Jews). They do not value the law as a revelation of the will of God but only as a device for establishing security for themselves.

God does not give the law, or any other gift, as a way for people to score points against each other. We cannot use our list of converts or of recipients of our charity as a claim for approval. People have every right to object to being used in such a way. The only basis for our claim to be accepted is the cross of Christ; and the cross is, in human terms, a sign of failure, not of successful marketing. We put our trust not in what we have succeeded in getting other people to do but in what Christ has done for us. That is the only success that has any effect for Paul; the cross is his only cause for boasting.

The cross of Christ, he states, is the sign that, as far I am concerned, the world has been crucified, and, as far as the world is concerned, I also have been crucified. I look at the world, and to me it is doomed; it is nailed up and its power is finished. World looks at me and sees me as it has seen Jesus, as a rejected, useless criminal. I can accept the fact that world rejects me, because my rejection is the same as that of Christ. I can reject the world's rejection of me, because world is powerless and without authority. So, the distinctions which the world values, such as circumcision and uncircumcision, no longer matter at all. A new creation has begun, and that is all that matters.

How do we recognise this new creation? It will not be detected by the systems of the world, it will be subversive of them. It will confuse the Security Police of religion and cultural conformity; they will not know what to look for, because it will not have the usual array of dogmas and manifestos and programmes which they are trained to detect. Those who are infected by the new creation will recognise each other, according to circumstances, not by any code that can be cracked by security but by silence, by a wink or a laugh or a tear, by suffering when there is no obvious point in suffering, or by a refusal to take something seriously; in a word, by their freedom.

The first Creation, according to the Scriptures, happened out of chaos. It was a kind of victory. The same is true of the new creation. It does not necessarily take place in the temple, or on a quiet hillside, or in a place of obvious success. The cross is the sign of new creation; it happens at the place of chaos, where the best law and the best religion and the voice of public opinion have been united in taking the side of injustice and prejudice, where people have turned their backs on the offer of freedom and have become slogan-shouters, and where truth is treated as an unnecessary luxury. It is out of such chaos and such dying that new creation may be expected, not in the Sabbath rest by Galilee but at the storm-centre of history at Jerusalem.

In such a situation, the agents of new creation develop a certain skill, not the skill to deflect chaos or to identify who is to blame, but a skill somehow to live through it and to discover the new amidst the wreck and loss of the old. This is the kind of discovery that Viktor Frankel was making among his colleagues at Auschwitz. But it is not such a rare experience as it may sound. Many people get a taste of it as they cope with personal tragedies. And, more corporately, a renewal of hope can happen when the people who have the power to make important statements and write portentous editorials just run out of words. It can happen when people discover that they are more than their traditional identities would allow them to be, when they can take responsibility for what they really are, rather than allowing their circumcised-ness or uncircumcised-ness to make their decisions for them.

This gospel of the cross is a line, a measure by which a design can be made firm; for those who walk according to this rule – the 'orthopods' – may there be peace and mercy, and upon all the children of Abraham.

The knowledge that we are reliably loved by God is our fundamental security; with it, we can venture into complete insecurity, living without landmarks or special badges of identity.

So, says Paul, let no one try to trouble or disturb me or shake my confidence – they won't succeed! I bear on my body the marks of Jesus. All the previous argument has been because of people who want to be distinguished by having the signs that they belong to a specific religious or cultural group. But there is no security in this; it merely produces groups and counter-groups, ideologies and counter-ideologies. But the new creation has come, which makes all that striving irrelevant. The new creation is the cross of Christ, the Christ in whom there is neither circumcised nor uncircumcised, neither Jew nor Gentile nor any other distinction, the Christ who loved me and gave himself for me. This gives me a security which no longer depends on my being separate from anybody, for this security is for all humanity. I belong to this Christ, and the only marks that matter to me are those that show that I belong to Christ. How exactly these are to be recognised, Paul does not specify. But the marks of Jesus are surely the marks made by the crucifixion.

When Deaf people wanted to find a sign for 'Jesus' in sign-language, there must have been many attractive possibilities – friend, saviour, lover, king, shepherd – all possible signs, all meaningful. But they in fact opted for the most simple and moving of all the signs, the marks of the nails. 'Jesus' in sign language is expressed by pointing with the middle finger of one hand to the centre of the palm of the other. The marks assure us that the death of Jesus was a real death; he was hurt, as any of us would be hurt by having a nail driven through our hand. He was not just God in disguise. If Jesus had been able to survive crucifixion without damage, this would not have been a miracle of salvation. It would have shown simply that here was the old divine superiority, and the ancient divide between God and the human being was still in place. The marks of Jesus show that the most fundamental apartheid has been overcome; there has been a real miracle, in which we humans can share. There has been a genuine victory over death, over all that separates us from each other, over the destructiveness of law and flesh and enslavement. They show that it is worth-while struggling for truth in the face of prejudice. It is worth-while claiming freedom in an enslaving world. And these marks are not reserved for Jesus so that we can worship him from afar; they are shared with his people, and are to be found in his body, his family.

Paul ends by claiming this blessing for his Galatian friends. These unfortunate, confused and anxious people whom he has rebuked and cajoled and lectured, they also share in this grace, the powerful, joyful grasp of Jesus Christ. There is no verb in this sentence. It is a prayer, that grace may be with them. It is also a statement, that grace is with them, and will be.

The next-to-last word is really unusual. No other document in the New Testament ends like this, with a word of address standing on its own, so emphatically. 'Brother-sisters' is Paul's final word; this is what he calls them; this is what they are, his brothers and sisters, each other's brothers and sisters, and brothers and sisters for us. This is the summary of the whole enterprise. This is the gospel of Jesus Christ.

The last word: Amen: yes, Lord. Yes indeed.

Our final prayer is Desmond Tutu's creed.[60]

Goodness is stronger than evil,	*Mae daioni yn gryfach na drygioni,*
Love is stronger than hate.	*Mae cariad yn gryfach na chasineb.*
Light is stronger than darkness,	*Mae goleuni yn gryfach na thywyllwch,*
Life is stronger than death.	*Mae bywyd yn gryfach nag angau.*
Victory is ours	*Mae buddugoliaeth gynnon ni*
Through him who loved us.	*Trwy'r hwn a'n carodd ni.*

References

1. Quoted in Edward Robinson, *The Language of Mystery* (London: SCM Press, 1987), p. 36.
2. J.B. Lightfoot, *Saint Paul's Epistle to the Galatians* (London: Macmillan, 1900), pp. 12-17.
3. Acts 11:26.
4. Psalms 95, 96, 98 etc.
5. Acts 2:4-11.
6. Genesis 11:1-9.
7. See Patrick Thomas, *A Candle in the Darkness* (Llandysul: Gomer Press, 1993), p. 72 and following chapters.
8. Acts 10:1-11, 18. See John D. Davies, 'Who Converts Whom?', in John Vincent (ed.), *Acts in Practice* (Blandford Forum: Deo Publishing, 2013), pp. 126-35.
9. 1 Corinthians 16:1-4; 2 Corinthians 8 and 9; Romans 15:25-28.
10. The Gaza Mobile Dental Clinic is funded by the Church in Wales's Jubilee Fund, set up by Archbishop Rowan Williams as a millennium project to support work in the land where Jesus was born 2,000 years ago. The Clinic is operated by the Near East Council of Churches, and works in the Shejaiyah District of Gaza City. In spite of heavy bombardment of that area, and the hazardous and impoverished conditions all around, it served 4,000 patients in 2014, who otherwise would have had no access to dental care. Patients come via the Family Health Centres run by the Council of Churches, in collaboration with the Al Ahli Hospital. The mobile clinic is clearly identified as a project funded by the Church in Wales. The Church aims to provide £20,000 a year to support this project. The Jubilee Fund is administered by the Church in Wales office at 39 Cathedral Road, Cardiff CF119XF (02920 348200) (info@churchinwales.org.uk).
11. Winston Halapua, *Waves of God's Embrace* (Norwich: Canterbury Press, 2008), p. 77. While presenting the case for concern about rising sea-levels, the Archbishop's main interest in this unique book is to offer an authoritative spirituality and theological language, based on the Pacific people's experience of the Ocean; a wonderful new world-view which should appeal to all peoples who, like the Welsh, have the sea and its mysteries as integral to their folk-memory.
12. Quotations from Martin Luther King Jr in this book are from a lecture which Dr King gave in St Louis in 1964. He gave us permission to distribute a recording on LP of this lecture in South Africa in 1966. It was immediately put on a banning order, which prohibited the playing of the record or listening to it. I kept a copy of this LP, the only one in England and Wales, which I have given to Gladstone's Library, Hawarden, where

it can be accessed. It is an inspiring summary of Dr King's primary messages, and has not otherwise been published.

13. John 16:13
14. Acts 6:1.
15. Acts 4:36.
16. Martin Luther, *Commentary on St Paul's Epistle to the Galatians* 1535 (London: James Clarke, 1953), pp. 179f.
17. George Firth, *The Plate-glass Prison* (London: RNID, 1966), p. 37.
18. Acts 8:9; 13:8
19. Matthew 2:1-12.
20. Genesis 12:1–4; Hebrews 11:8-19.
21. D. Bonhoeffer, *The Cost of Discipleship* (London: SCM Press, 1959), p. 117.
22. Acts 2:36.
23. For what it's worth, I have got mine down as far as a granddaughter of Charlemagne, who married a Baldwin, who brought his name to Trefaldwyn, which may account for my sense of affinity with Sir Drefaldwyn/Montgomeryshire; but, that far back, everyone is related to everyone else.
24. Matthew 1:1-17; Luke 3:23-38.
25. D. Gwenallt Jones, *Eples* (Llandysul: Gomer Press, 1951), p. 64.
26. Story told by Edward Robinson, artist and sculptor.
27. See essays about land-tenure in Leviticus by John Vincent and John Davies, in John Rogerson (ed.), *Leviticus in Practice*, Blandford Forum: Deo Publishing, 2014.
28. Because of my interest in the concerns of Deaf people, I was once asked to become Chairman of the Church of England Council for the Deaf; I refused, on the grounds that the post ought to be taken by a Deaf person. But they found another hearing bishop to do the job!
29. Many of the concerns mentioned in this paragraph are developed more thoroughly in Wayne Morris, *Theology without Words*, Aldershot: Ashgate, 2008.
30. Trevor Huddleston, *Naught for your Comfort* (London: Collins Fontana), p. 51.
31. Saunders Lewis, *Buchedd Garmon*, Aberystwyth: Gwasg Aberystwyth, 1937.
32. This translation, and the explanation of the play given in the following paragraph, are quoted from personal correspondence from Saunders Lewis to myself.
33. H.J. Hammerton, *This Turbulent Priest* (London: Lutterworth Press, 1952), pp. 75, 107.
34. See note 12 above.
35. Romans 15:7.
36. D. Bonhoeffer, *Life Together* (London: SCM Press, 1954), p. 17.
37. C.K. Barrett, *Freedom and Obligation* (London, SPCK, 1985), p. 42.
38. Noted by Wayne Morris, see above.
39. D. Bonhoeffer, *Life Together*, p. 84.
40. Exodus 2:1-10.

41. Sir Henry Morton Stanley, *The Autobiography of Sir Henry Morton Stanley*, Santa Barbara: Narrative Press, 1909

42. John 19:25-27.

43. Jonathan Sacks, *The Great Partnership* (London: Hodder & Stoughton, 2011), p. 8. See Genesis 21:1-19.

44. Romans 5:2; Ephesians 2:18; 3:12.

45. Mark 11:1-11.

46. Isaiah 19:23-25. See also Psalm 87, and Jim Cotter's glorious extension of Psalm 87 in his *Psalms for a Pilgrim People* (New York: Morehouse Publishing, 1998), pp. 185f.

47. Luke 19:41-44.

48. In 2002, the International Eisteddfod at Llangollen was overwhelmed by an extraordinary, racially inclusive, youth choir from the Western Cape, South Africa, called Pro Cantu. It been in existence for only five years, the creation of a young conductor called André van der Merwe. With its sheer brilliance, the inclusiveness of its repertoire, its disciplined passion, it came first in almost every competition it entered for; it won the Choir of the World, where it was competing against some of the best adult choirs in the world. It disclosed the wealth of human resources which the apartheid system had been suppressing. Its account of Michael Tippett's version of Deep River spoke with unforgettable authority. This was Freedom.

49. Deuteronomy 10:19; 15:15 etc.

50. Viktor Frankel, *Man's Search for Meaning* (London: Rider, 2004), p. 75. The whole book is testimony to the possibility of freedom within the conditions of Auschwitz.

51. Desmond Tutu, *God has a Dream* (London: Rider, 2004), p. 117.

52. 1 Corinthians 15:58.

53. 2 Peter 3:12.

54. Martin Luther's *Commentary on Galatians* (see note 12 above), pp. 483f.

55. Saint Augustine, *Confessions*, translated by R.S. Pine-Coffin (Harmondsworth: Penguin, 1961), p. 30.

56. See note 12 above.

57. Elias Chacour, *Faith Beyond Despair* (Norwich: Canterbury Press, 2008), p. 112. The whole book is testimony to the possibilities of making peace in defiance of an environment which obstructs peace at every turn.

58. This could be the most significant question in this series of questions suggested in this book; it picks up the issue which was fundamental in St Paul's purpose in writing his Letter. Probably, most of us can think of things which have been added to the fundamental faith in Christ, things which may have value but which may have been divisive or exclusive. In my youth, this for me was the fastidious in-group apparatus of Anglo-Catholic devotion. At the same time, I was struck by the exclusiveness of some understandings of 'being sound'. For others, it may be an in-group commitment to certain types or standards of music. When, over the last thirty years or so, I have asked students of *Galatians* this question, the most common reply has been 'the charismatic movement' – this from some who have been deeply appreciative of that movement's blessings. Almost

anything which is good in itself can be co-opted into a movement for
exclusion.

59. Luke 4:1-13.

60. Archbishop Desmond Tutu, adapted by John Bell, with music, in *There is
One Among Us* (John L. Bell, the Wild Goose Worship Group, The Iona
Community, Glasgow, 1995), p. 30.

Other titles published in the Practice Interpretation series:

1. John Vincent, ed., *The Stilling of the Storm*, ISBN 978-1-905679-17-1
2. John Vincent, ed., *Acts in Practice*, ISBN 978-1-905679-28-7
3. John Rogerson, ed., *Leviticus in Practice*, ISBN 978-1-905679-24-9
4. John Vincent, ed., *The Farewell Discourses in Practice*, ISBN 978-1-905679-33-1

All titles available from the publisher.